THE SIEGE OF O'OKIEP

(GUERRILLA CAMPAIGN IN THE ANGLO-BOER WAR)

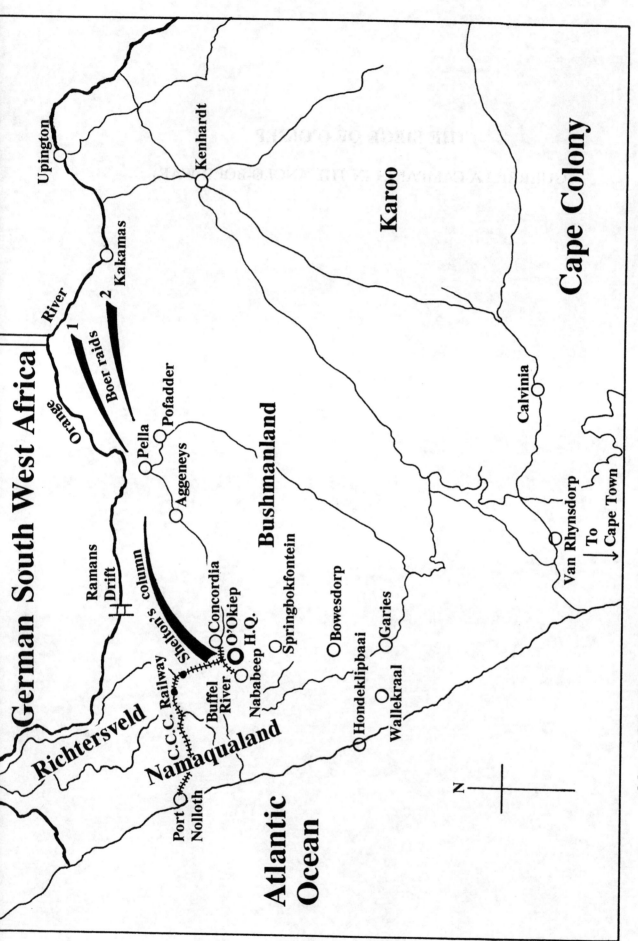

Map of Cape Colony showing North West area around British Headquarters at O'Okiep and direction to East of Shelton's mobile columns to engage Boer Commando troops near Pella and Aggeneys (1) 2 March 1901 and (2) July 1902.

German South West Africa

Richtersveld

Namaqualand

Atlantic Ocean

Bushmanland

Karoo

Cape Colony

Upington

Kenhardt

Kakamas

Orange River

Boer raids

1

2

Pofadder

Pella

Aggeneys

Ramans Drift

Shelton's column

Concordia

O'Okiep H.Q.

Nababeep

C.C.C. Railway

Buffel River

Springbokfontein

Bowesdorp

Garies

Hondeklipbaai

Wallekraal

Port Nolloth

Calvinia

Van Rhynsdorp

To Cape Town

N

PETER BURKE

THE SIEGE OF O'OKIEP

(GUERRILLA CAMPAIGN IN THE ANGLO-BOER WAR)

WAR MUSEUM OF THE BOER REPUBLICS
BLOEMFONTEIN, REPUBLIC OF SOUTH AFRICA
1995

War Museum of the Boer Republics
P.O. Box 704
Bloemfontein, Republic of South Africa

ISBN 1-874979-01-4

Printed by *N.G. Sendingpers*, P.O. Box 19, Bloemfontein
Republic of South Africa

"For Carol, for typing the original manuscript many times during difficult periods of extensive research and for Christopher, Michelle and Phillippa without whose understanding and help this book would not have been possible."

Photograph, Dust Jacket : Lieutenant Colonel W.S. Shelton

CONTENTS

CONTENTS

FOREWORD

In 1940 when I was ten years old I was living in Hayle, Cornwall and noticed the name O'Okiep[1] etched in gold plate over the doorway of a grocer's shop where I collected the rations for my family. It was a strange coincidence that many years later the account of the Siege of O'Okiep in the form of the Colonel's diary came into my possession.

The following account is a true story based on the official Staff Diary, private papers, documents and unique photographs of Lieutenant Colonel W.S. Shelton DSO of the 3rd Battalion 'The Queens' Royal West Surrey Regiment and original Boer letters and messages, these include three valuable letters from General Jan Smuts.

All these documents are now published for the first time.

The story covers the last eighteen months of the guerrilla campaign during those dark days of the Anglo-Boer War, (1899-1902), or the 2nd War of Independance as the Afrikaner knows it and brings back an era of South African and British Empire history -sometimes forgotten today.

In January 1901 Sir Alfred Milner, Governor of the Cape Colony, appointed Colonel Shelton of the 3rd Bn., The Queens Royal Regiment, to be Commandant of Namaqualand which is situated in the remote area of the North-West Cape, South Africa, just below the Orange River. The district is the second largest in South Africa and it was Shelton's job to protect its 17,000 square miles from Boer infiltration. In addition to the main properties in the district are the important Copper Mining Towns of O'Okiep, Concordia and Nababeep. The valuable mines were worked and maintained by Cornish miners and engineers who had emigrated to that district in the 1850's during the recession in the copper and tin industries in Cornwall. They brought with them their traditions and way of life, some of which has survived to this day. The town was served from the west coast, Port Nolloth, by a narrow gauge railway, ninety-one and a half miles long, which was vulnerable to attack by Boer commando.

In March 1901 Shelton's district was awakened to the grim aspects of war when commando troops begin raiding his North-Eastern area as a preliminary to the classic trip made by General Smuts into the British held Cape Colony from his starting point in the Eastern Transvaal. It was the most troublesome time for the British Military Authorities. Colonel Shelton's main problem was his lack of fully trained troops and experienced officers - although Sir Alfred Milner was supporting him where he could. General Smuts advances bringing with him additional 'Volunteers' as he evades the British Army Patrols who search for him and his men throughout the open veld. In

---

1. **Publisher's Note:** The current version of spelling of place names has been used throughout the text thus sometimes resulting in a difference between the text and the original documents. The 1902 spelling of O'Okiep(also O'OKiep,O'okiep,OOkiep and o'okiep), for instance, is now Okiep and, apart from the keeping of the old form in the foreword, the modern version is used in the text in the rest of the book. Where documents are directly quoted the original spelling is used., but in the text it was decided to use the modern version to enable tourists and researchers to effectively use currently available maps.

April 1902, with a superior force of commandos, Smuts encircles and attacks the Copper Mining Towns individually. Shelton has made O'Okiep, the largest of these towns, his HQ, and with the Superintendent of the Cape Copper Company (Major Dean) he has fortified the Settlement with thirteen blockhouses and miles of barbed wire. In addition Shelton raised Namaqualand Border scouts and trained Town Guards (all volunteers) to protect the properties from the Boers. His Garrison was strengthened by half a company of the 5th Battalion Royal Warwickshire Regiment who have fallen back on O'Okiep after being cut off by Boers in Shelton's Southern area near Garies.

The story unfolds further into dramatic consequences for Shelton and his Garrison (including 5,500 women and children) when O'Okiep is isolated and completely cut off from the outside world by General Smuts and his men who are determined to take the town as their main prize.

* * *

ACKNOWLEDGEMENTS

The author would like to thank the following people and organisations who have helped in his research and given every assistance during the preparation of this book.

The South African High Commissioner, London. Also Mr H.W. Short of this Office.

The staff of the Reference Library of South Africa House in London, especially the librarian, Ms Yvonne Baker.

Mr W.C. Watson of the Director General of Surveys Office in Pretoria, South Africa.

Mr S.J. Schoeman of the Government Archives, Cape Town, South Africa.

The Regional Director (Western Cape) of the Cape Town Post Office.

The Company Secretary, Mr P.E. Hyland and Board of the Okiep Copper Company, Nababeep, Cape Province, for their kind co-operation and answering my many questions over the past years.

Mr D.B. Olmesdahl, Historian of the Post Office Museum, Pretoria, South Africa.

The National Army Museum (Department of Uniforms), London.

The Hydrographic Office, Ministry of Defence (navy), Taunton, Somerset, for allowing me to reproduce the Port Nolloth harbour area and sea approach from one of their charts.

The Librarian, South African Railways Reference Library, Johannesburg, South Africa.

Union Castle Line (The British & Commonwealth Shipping Company PLC), London.

Sir W. Hancock - Canberra University, Australia.

Regional Director - Department of Posts and Telecommunications of the Republic of South Africa.

Chief of the South African Defence HQ, Pretoria, South Africa.

Major P.G.E. Hill of the Queens Royal West Surrey Regiment Museum, Clandon Park, West Clandon, Guildford, Surrey.

The South African Library, Cape Town.

I would also like to thank Major Jock Haswell (rtd) of the Royal West Surrey Regiment "The Queens" for reading through my early manuscript and making useful suggestions.

And lastly -
I hasten to apologise to any person or organisation who I may have forgotten to include in the above acknowledgements.

Peter Burke   Ruislip, 1995

CHAPTER 1

TO THE SEAT OF THE WAR

The Anglo-Boer War began on the 11th October, 1899, when they invaded Natal. By the 4th July, 1900, their forces had been decisively defeated in the field and Field Marshal Lord Roberts, the British Commander-in-Chief, assumed that, to all intents and purposes, the war was over. He therefore handed over to Lord Kitchener, and, with General Sir Redvers Buller, returned to England. In fact, the Boers had no intention of accepting defeat and, with highly mobile commandos and guerrilla tactics, opened a new phase of the war which finally ended with the siege of Okiep by General J.C. Smuts in March, April and May 1902, and the Treaty of Vereeniging on the 31st May, 1902. Under the terms of this treaty the Orange Free State and Transvaal became part of British South Africa. The Union of South Africa was established eight years later in 1910.

As so often before, the Boer advance into Natal took the British Government by surprise, and during hasty mobilisation in England the 3rd Battalion of The Queen's Royal Regiment, a militia unit, was raised on the 4th December, 1899. On the 20th February, 1900 it paraded at Cambridge Barracks, Portsmouth, for a brief address by the Commanding Officer, Lieutenant Colonel Fairtlough, before embarking on SS *Cephalonia* for Cape Town, where it arrived on the 27th March.

The Second-in- Command was Major W.S. Shelton who was subsequently to be awarded the Distinguished Service Order for his defence of Okiep in Namaqualand, in the extreme north-west of Cape Colony.

On arrival in Cape Town the battalion was sent to the British communications centre and supply depot at De Aar, and manned outposts in the vicinity. In May 1900 it was dispersed over a wide area to protect the main railway line to Mafeking. Major Shelton was appointed Commandant of the district known as Victoria West.

By the middle of 1900, British forces had occupied Bloemfontein and Pretoria and had raised the sieges of Mafeking, Ladysmith and Kimberley. In October, the 3rd Battalion of the Queen's returned to Cape Town and was employed in guarding Boer prisoners-of-war at Green Point. It was while he was at Green Point that Major Shelton was told to report to the Castle in Cape Town for special duty.

On January 15th, 1901, Major Shelton arrived at the Castle in Cape Town where he was informed that His Excellency the High Commissioner, Sir Alfred Milner wished to see him. He went at once to Government House where Captain Lampton (Military Secretary) greeted him saying that the High Commissioner wished him to stay to lunch as there was much to discuss regarding a far off and remote area called Namaqualand. Shelton remained with Milner for over three hours during which time the High Commissioner went into great detail regarding a special job he wished Shelton to carry out. Milner stressed the vital importance of the valuable copper mining property in Namaqualand and his object was to send Shelton to this area to organize a strong defence force for the protection of this valuable centre, the railway and Port Nolloth. He assured Shelton that he would do all in his power to assist him should difficulties arise. One of the major problems he had was in obtaining officers to go with him and on this point Milner promised he would find someone suitable. A day later Shelton received a letter from Milner saying he had succeeded in persuading a Mr Gamble to go to Namaqualand as an Intelligence Officer.

The telegraph wires had already been cut by a Boer commando unit under the command of General C. De Wet, this was the earliest raid into the British Colony by the Boers, although two Commanders, J.B.M. Hertzog and P.H. Kritzinger, were too weak in number to hold off the British troops they encountered. De Wet's unit was consequently scattered before they could retire back across the Orange River. De Wet himself was fortunate enough to escape but he lost the majority of his commando. They had hoped to obtain strong support from the sympathetic Dutch community living in the Cape but unfortunately they received little reaction. Following this premature raid into British territory, the British military quickly organized Town Guards which would be capable of supporting the regular troops who were often hard pressed to operate on mobile columns over a vast area. Some days before Major Shelton was due to leave for Namaqualand he was promoted to Honorary Lieutenant Colonel.

Although he did not realize at the time of this new appointment, Shelton was about to embark on one of the most difficult jobs of his entire military career. He was also

The 3rd Bn on route to Cape Town on S.S. Cephalonia.
Note the Queen's' badge on the diamond-shaped cloth
attached to the pugri of the kakhi helmet.

destined to play a major role in an important historical episode of the South African campaign. At midnight on the 20th January, 1901, the military commandant arrived in the important copper mining town of Okiep after a tiring sea and land journey. He was greeted by Major Dean, Captain of the Cape Copper Company, and various local dignitaries who were delighted to see him. Colonel Shelton quickly assumed command of the district.

In order to appreciate the herculean task that lay ahead of Shelton, it is necessary to understand some facts about Namaqualand at the time he was made commandant. This arid and desolate district is situated in the far off north-west corner of the Cape Colony and covers 17,500 square miles. It is bounded on the north by the Orange River (the Gariep, the Hottentot name for the River of the Wilderness) and the neutral German South-West African territory. On the east the waterless and inhospitable Bushmanland. To the south the district of Vanrhynsdorp and the west by the vast Atlantic Ocean where the extremely cold 'Benguela currents' sweep northwards along the coast from which the aridity of Namaqualand is governed. The entire population of the district was 17,000 - many of whom were concentrated in the mining area around Okiep. The name Namaqualand is taken from the plural of 'Nama' which name originates from the large Hottentot tribes - a nomadic people of the area - who had lived there many years before

Men of 3rd Queen's after coaling
on board SS Cephalonia

white men had settled in South Africa. The Namaqua tribe of Hottentots migrated north into South-West Africa during the beginning of the 1800's, and left evidence in the names they used to describe characteristics of the Namaqualand terrain with its many contrasts. In 1901 Namaqualand was already world famous for its large production of rich copper ore, and a great variety of flowers and rare species of succulent plants.

It was in the mid 1920's that Namaqualand again was featured throughout South Africa and the world when diamonds were discovered along the North-West Coast near the Orange River. Namaqualand's coast is a sandy desert stretching some thirty miles inland where it gradually gives way to a rugged plateau of barren mountains which vary in altitude from 2,000 feet to well over 4,000 feet above sea level. This hardvelt is a formation of mountainous country separating the coastal strip from the inland areas which is spread right along the South African territory.

The first task for Shelton was to send a full report to Sir Alfred Milner and General Settle in Cape Town which was to show all local information of the Copper Mining area, population and type of terrain. Strategic data was of the utmost importance, as was the aspect of communication, transport, availability of water and forage. General Settle was in charge of all land communication and supplies and it was imperative he received Shelton's report quickly. Shelton lost no time in appointing local officers and NCO's to form Town Guards and Border Scouts for defence of the copper mining area and the important link of communication - the small gauge railway line to Port Nolloth.

3rd Battalion Queen's boarding train to De Aar

3rd Queen's Regiment escort Boer prisoners

3rd Queen's march through the town Beaufort West

3rd Queen's Church Parade at Beaufort West.

Drums 3rd Queen's beating retreat, Beaufort West.

10

Detraining at De Aar - 3rd Bn. Queen's Royal West Surrey Regt.

3rd Queen's guarding the railway.

11

Shelton managed to get his dispatch off to Cape Town by the quickest possible route via the Port on the steamer *Nautilus* which called at the Port every month using also the German vessel *Gertrude Woermann*. The British Commandant had carefully compiled his information with the help of the field intelligence department, sending Sir Alfred Milner, and his General, the following news;-

"The town of O'OKiep is the Headquarters of the Cape Copper Company and Namaqualand Field Force, and is situated ninety-one and a half miles by rail from Port Nolloth. The estimated value of the working mines is £600,000. Number of inhabitants 2,000 of which 450 are white. Nearly all are employees of the above Company. The town is built in a hollow and surrounded on the north side and west by high hills. To the south the ground slopes upwards gently away from the town. To the north-east and east the hills are 'kopjes' and are close to, and command the town which is spread out - some of the houses being 500 to 600 yards away close under the hills. It is an ideal town to attack and could only be held against an enemy with artillery by a very large force. I have formed a Town Guard of nine officers and 328 NCO's and men, also there is an exterior line of defence - a chain of outposts (blockhouses) completely encircling the mining town with troops of the Garrison on duty."

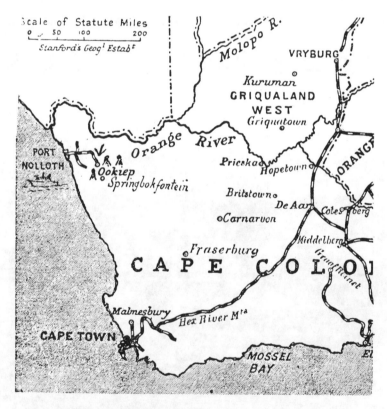

Map showing position of Okiep Copper Mines, N.W. Cape Colony, South Africa

Sir Alfred Milner & His Staff. Alfred Milner was born in Giessen, Hesse-Darmstadt (West Germany) on March 23rd, 1854. He was a brillaint academic completing his education at Oxford. In 1897 the British Colonial Secretary Joseph Chamberlain, sent him to South Africa as High Commissioner where his uncompromising administration was to antagonize President Kruger and his Boer leaders.

13

Shelton's guns were mounted on Fort Shelton (north of the town) and manned by the Cape Garrison Artillery (C.G.A.)

A second, or interior line of strongly entrenched positions occupied by men of the Town Guard covered the Waterworks, Mines and the majority of the houses. Barbed wire entanglements completely surrounded the town, constituting a major obstacle to a determined advance by the enemy.

Shelton had over 380,000 lbs of wheat, meal and flour in the food stores of the Garrison Headquarters. At Nababeep (a neighbouring town) there was at least 160,00 lbs of bread and material which could be brought into Okiep if necessary. At Steinkopf (a German missionary station to the north), the Minister, Revd E. Beisenback, had offered to supply Shelton with 300 bags of wheat at 21 shillings a bag. Fresh meat was in ample supply in the neighbourhood with much live-stock available - unless Okiep was completely cut off. There was no grass or veldt within 18 miles of the mining town. Shelton's other essential supplies were ample at the time he assumed command of the district.

Maxim Machine Gun near Beaufort West

14

Water - one of the most important commodities, was in good supply and was pumped from the mine. Shelton was to put this to good use later in this campaign. The rainfall in the district was very small and an average amount over the previous 12 years before Shelton's arrival was 7.076 inches, the most in one month being 1.29 inches. Communication by the railway to Port Nolloth on the Atlantic Coast was vital. The Cape Copper Company owned the line which ran through rugged terrain for ninety-one and a half miles over the highest mountain peak at Klipfontein to the sea port. It had cost the Copper Company £250,000 to build, and was two feet six inches gauge. The Company ran eight locomotives and special passenger carriages including a brake van which was essential when descending from the high ground. Various other rolling stock included 57 buck wagons which were all in use to the mining area carrying 4,000 pounds in weight in each wagon. Shelton had plenty of forage for the animals, which included 62 mules on the Cape Copper Company railway, plus 56 in Okiep. His supply would be sufficient for 3 months.

The general communication of the vast district was by road which were not that good and became greatly damaged by any rainfall which removed the hard core base.   The

Captain Wilkinson on duty - Beaufort West

Boers had actually cut the telegraph lines on January 18th, 1901 but this had now been restored.

There was a 'Post Cart' from Okiep to join the railway in the south at Piketberg Road, which took 72 hours, passing through the towns of Springbokfontein, Bowesdorp, Garies and Clanwilliam. Apart from the railway to Port Nolloth there were the two steamers *Nautilus* and the German *Gertrude Woermann,* but Shelton reported that neither of these ships could be depended on, as to time, and he thought he would be far better served by *HMS Magpie* which Sir Alfred Milner had arranged to call at the Port regularly for Shelton's messages. Other towns in the neighbourhood of Okiep were Springbokfontein, Concordia and Nababeep. Springbokfontein about 5 miles south of Okiep was the Headquarters of the Resident Magistrate and had a jail. There was a mine there, but not working, also a telegraph office, population 170 including 70 whites. Nababeep lies about 7 miles to the west of Okiep and is the site of one of the Cape Copper Company's mines.

Captain Walker 3rd Bn Queen's inspecting sentry, Lines of Communication

The Town Guard consisted of 3 officers, 126 NCO's and men. Population 100 whites and 1,400 coloured. It is joined by the railway line from Braakputs junction where it then runs to the Port. This link line cost the Cape Copper Company £13,000.

Concordia lies some 7 miles to the north-east of Okiep and is the Headquarters of the Namaqua Copper Company. The value of the working mine there is £200,000. Population 2,200 including 100 whites (this also accounts for natives living in the vicinity). A Town Guard under the command of Captain Phillips J.P. had been formed there. Strength 5 officers and N.C.O's and 215 men. Drill instructors go over from HQ Okiep twice a week to drill the men.

Railway communicates with the Cape Copper Company line at Braakputs, which is about one and a half miles north of Okiep. Line cost £5,000. Mules haul trucks to link up at the main junction thence to Port Nolloth by rail. Water supply is just enough for the inhabitants. Port Nolloth is the sea port for Namaqualand. The distance by sea to Cape Town is 285 miles. The Port is an extremely hazardous one for landing owing to a dangerous bar off the Port. This can delay the landing of passengers for as many as 5 or 6 days. The chief trade at the Port is the shipment of copper ore by the two mining companies, Cape Copper Company and Namaqua Copper Company. The population is 350 whites and about 1,000 coloured. The water is brought in tanks by rail from a pumping station 5 miles away on the Okiep railway.

On January 19th, a Town Guard was formed under the command of the Resident Magistrate G.E. Syme Esq., with two officers and 125 NCO's and men. A sergeant of regular forces was appointed as drill instructor.

Here, a series of six entrenched positions were constructed entirely by the Town Guard and Convict Labour, under the supervision of the Captain of *HMS Magpie* and the ship landed 2 Nordenfeldt guns with an officer and 6 men to assist in the defence of the port. In addition to this, an armoured truck patrolled the railway line as far as the waterworks 5 miles out. Further than that the entire railway was guarded by the armed men of the Namaqualand Border Scouts (2nd Battalion). Mr Symes was also the Customs Officer and Port Captain. Also in the district of Namaqualand were the towns of Garies, Bowesdorp, Nuwerus, Hondeklip Bay, Spektakel, Komaggas, Leliefontein and Pella. Colonel Shelton was also greatly assisted by the other Resident Magistrate at Springbokfontein, Mr J.B. Van Renen, while carrying out his duties and enforcing 'Martial Law' throughout the district.

Proclamation of King Edward VII at O'OKiep, Namaqualand

18

Since the arrival of Shelton in Okiep he had received a great deal of valuable help from the Chief Superintendent of the Cape Copper Company, Mr J.L. Dean, who was appointed Major in command of the Okiep Town Guard. Major Dean had been indefatigable - literally working night and day. The whole of the defence works, with the exception of the Field Gun emplacement, had been constructed by the employees of the Cape Copper Company under Major Dean's supervision. The barbed wire (13 miles of it) was procured from Cape Town entirely at the Company's expense, with the entanglements erected by the Company's men. The whole of the arms, ammunition, guns, equipment and supplies from Cape Town had been forwarded by rail from Port Nolloth 'free of charge'.

Colonel Shelton concluded his report to Cape Town by commenting;

> "I have no hesitation in saying there is a minimum of disloyalty in the district. The Community in this area and Port Nolloth is essentially English. I believe the farmers to be loyal and the 'Bastards' are loyal to the core, and form a formidable backbone to the fighting element of this district."

Description of 'Bastards': Natives of the district descended from Hottentot women and early Dutch settlers. They object to being called 'Hottentots' and prefer to be called 'Bastards'.

Colonel Shelton now made plans to appoint his staff for the Garrison Headquarters; Lieutenant Gamble to be Staff Officer, with local rank of Captain, Lieutenant Caldow to be Intelligence Officer (subject to confirmation by Commanding Officer Supplies Land Communications). A small detachment of Cape Town Highlanders, having already arrived at Okiep was also taken on the strength. Lieutenant Mills and 10 NCO's and men Cape Town Highlanders, Sergeant Campbell, Sergeant Rollandson, Sergeant Pipfield (drill instructors), Private Collins, 3rd Queen's Regiment, Commandants Servant.

Martial Law was quickly proclaimed throughout the district, thereby suspending civil law and no one was allowed to travel in Namaqualand without a pass signed by the military Commandant of issued by his deputies at the following towns who were; Okiep, Lieutenant J. Caldow I.O.; Port Nolloth, G. E. Syme R.M.; Concordia, F Phillips Esq., J.P.; Springbok, J.H. Van Renen Esq., C.C. & R.M.,Garies, Ernest Loynes Esq.; Anenous, N.E. Moffat Esq. J.P. The deputies were also given the power to censor letters and telegrams - to use telegraph offices at discretion and to remove explosives to a place of safety, but they were not empowered to make any terms with the enemy in case of surrender of their respective charges.

In addition to the volunteers in these towns Shelton raised a strong force of 'Border scouts' as his district was so large it was essential for him to send these men out into the

'Waterless' areas to ferret out and engage any Boer units. These troops were also known as Okiep Border Scouts who were mainly local men and knew the wilderness very well. They were to prove of invaluable assistance to the British Commandant in his great task.

The general title of the troops who were raised to defend the mining towns was The Namaqualand Town Guards. Shelton had studied the entire area very carefully especially from a strategic aspect when making Okiep his district Headquarters, which was the centre of the active copper mining properties, also it was served by the Cape Copper Company railway from Port Nolloth, with the branch lines to the neighbouring towns.

While all this defence organisation was taking place in Namaqualand, thousands of miles away at Osborne House in England, the great Queen Victoria was dying. It was at 6.30 pm (London time) on January 22nd, 1901, that her life finally came to an end. Her death was to close the greatest chapter in the history of the British Empire. The news of Her Majesty's death was quickly reported to the world, but it did not reach Okiep until some days after. In fact, late on the evening of Monday, January 26th, the news of the Queen's death reached Shelton in Okiep, having been brought by dispatch boat to Port Nolloth and then wired to the Commandant who immediately gathered his officers and all local dignitaries to tell them the sad news. A deep gloom was cast over all the town and neighbouring area. Shelton ordered that all flags should be flown at

Group of officers 3rd Queens - Colonel Shelton on right

half mast and black arm bands were to be worn by each officer and NCO of the Town Guards and Border Scouts. The mourning was visible throughout the entire district with the Commandant arranging a ceremonial parade for Wednesday, January 28th, with a full muster of the entire garrison. The open air memorial service was attended by the Commanding Officer, all his officers and staff, plus all members of the Cape Copper Company and inhabitants of the surrounding towns. Even the local natives of the district came to pay homage and respect to the great Queen Victoria. The local band played Handel's Dead March and the service was conducted by the Rev. C. F. Tobias. Although the grief felt by all was apparent, the Border scouts had no relaxation from their duty, and there was no doubt of the loyalty of every man, woman and child to the new King, Edward VII.

The Town Guards, already having been appointed for Okiep were Major J. L. Dean, who was also Superintendent of the Cape Copper Company, Captains F. A. Evans, J. Crozier, G. A. Burke, Lieutenants A. E. Thompson, E. H. Hodge, H. Willman, Medical Officer Dr R. N. Howard and non-commissioned Officer, Regimental Sergeant Major A. E. Gyngell, Quarter Master Sergeant H. A. H. Lewis, Colour Sergeants C. H. Jagger, W. Whittaker, T. H. Whiley, Sergeants R. Clacher, F. F. Middleweek, F. S. Nicholls, E. O. Whear, J. Burrows, W. Holt, C. A. Jones, W. J. Millett, T. Hannaford, R. H. Pellow, P. Thompson and W. W. Townsend Jnr.

A few days later on February 2nd, Shelton ordered the garrison of Okiep to parade as strong as possible at 4pm on Monday, February 4th, to celebrate the accession of His Majesty King Edward VII and for the promulgation of His Excellency the Governor's proclamation of His Majesty's accession to the throne. All inhabitants of the district were also invited to attend. As news of the accession of the new King circulated the district, Colonel Shelton began formulating his plans for the defence of the copper mining town and neighbouring mines. His problem was going to be the vast area which had to be protected against a Boer infiltration. Already, British Intelligence was gathering information which indicated a decisive move against the British held Cape Colony by a senior Boer general.

Following the occupation of Pretoria by the British the Boer leaders decided it would be impossible to continue fighting as one large army. After serious discussions the Boers agreed to break their army up into small commando units which could then strike at the enemy over a greater area. This unanimous agreement was approved by President Kruger at Waterval Boven. The new guerrilla warfare was about to begin and with it the greatest period and the hardest type of conflict for both sides. The Commando Units were allocated to various areas in which to operate. Their supplies of ammunition, food and clothing were to be obtained from the land and what they could possibly capture from the British Army which was rapidly becoming stronger every month as they continued to bring more troops and equipment to South Africa. One of the commando units was led by a brilliant politician who had become, through necessity, a soldier on the veldt. His name was Jan Christian Smuts. This man was to become one of the greatest and most respected gentlemen of our time. He was also regarded by many of the Boers as the main commando leader. Smuts had been born in the South-Western Cape, on a farm which was situated three miles from Riebeck West and he knew the area well. It had been decided that Smuts was to invade the British held Cape Colony and this

Funeral Parade - 3rd Queen's Bn

3rd Bn Queen's at Church Parade and Service

Colonel Shelton (seated third left) with some members of his Town Guard, February 1901 - note these men are wearing black arm band in mourning for Queen Victoria

Sheltering from a dust storm

23

meant a hazardous trek of some 2,000 miles from where he was to set out from Vereeniging in the east. In fact, this great journey was to prove to be one of the classic feats of the war, and most troublesome for the British.

By March, 1901, Shelton had completed his defence preparations in the district as far as possible with the men available to him. It was not going to be very long now before these defensive arrangements were to be put to the test by General Smuts and his experienced and rugged commando units.

Commanding Officer, Adjutant and Sergeants, 3rd Queen's

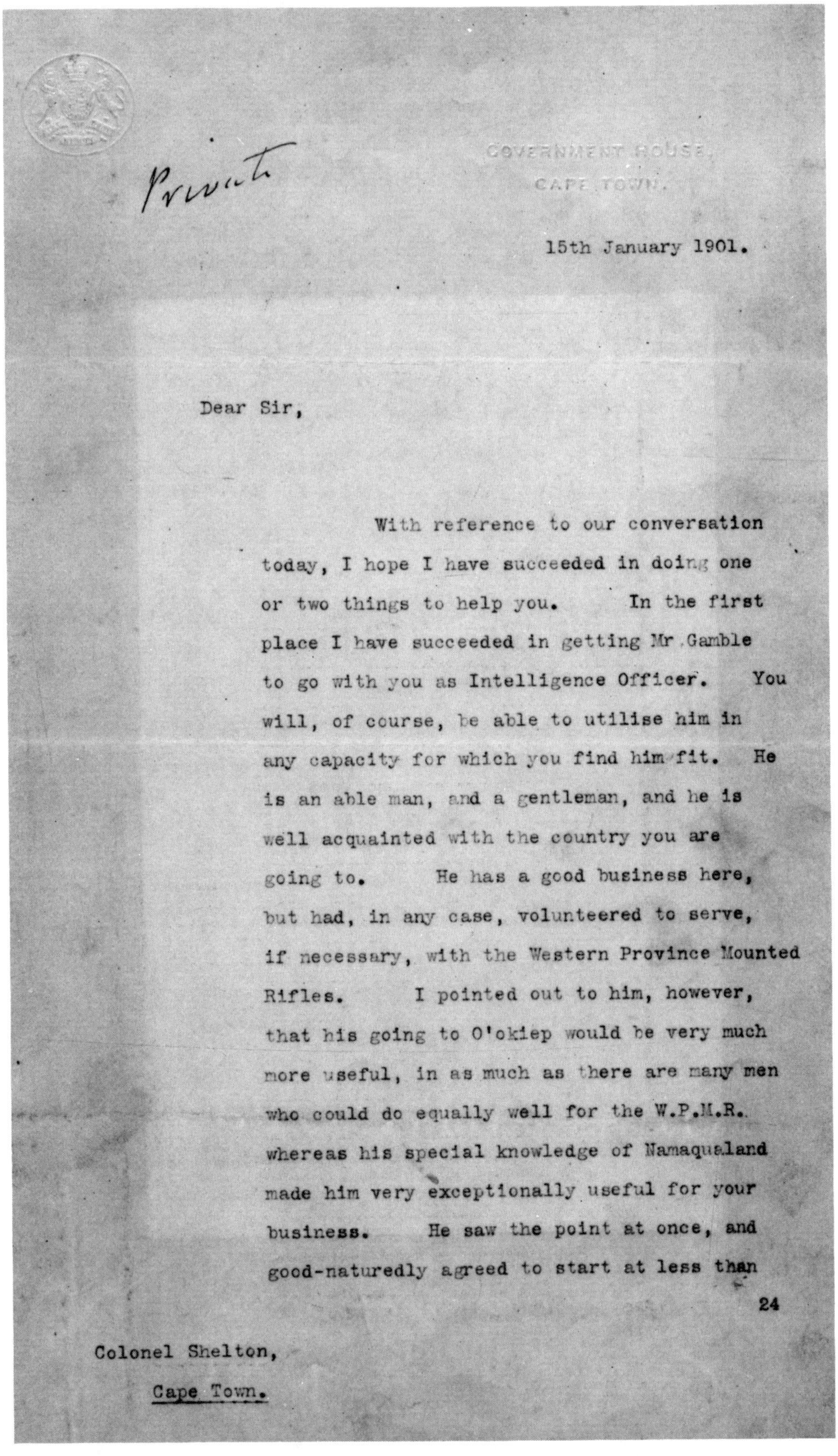

Private

15th January 1901.

Dear Sir,

With reference to our conversation today, I hope I have succeeded in doing one or two things to help you.   In the first place I have succeeded in getting Mr.Gamble to go with you as Intelligence Officer.   You will, of course, be able to utilise him in any capacity for which you find him fit.   He is an able man, and a gentleman, and he is well acquainted with the country you are going to.   He has a good business here, but had, in any case, volunteered to serve, if necessary, with the Western Province Mounted Rifles.   I pointed out to him, however, that his going to O'okiep would be very much more useful, in as much as there are many men who could do equally well for the W.P.M.R. whereas his special knowledge of Namaqualand made him very exceptionally useful for your business.   He saw the point at once, and good-naturedly agreed to start at less than

24

Colonel Shelton,

Cape Town.

Page 1 of original letter from Lord Milner to Colonel Shelton
(Author's collection)

24 hours notice.

The Intelligence Department propose
to send him in addition to the man whom you
mentioned today, and whom they had already
selected.   I think this is as well, for you
are so short-handed that you may as well take
any useful men you can get, but I think that
if there is any question as between the two,
Gamble, who is the better class man, should
be superior.

Secondly, the Admiral has kindly
consented to let the gunboat "Magpie", which
is patrolling the Western coast, call regularly
at Port Nolloth for your messages.   Whenever
you have anything to send she will take it
direct to Lamberts Bay, where a cruiser is
stationed, and the S.N.O. there will send it
on at once in a torpedo boat to Saldanha Bay
or St Helena Bay according to the weather.
There are telegraphic offices at both these
places, from which the messages will be sent
direct to Cape Town.   This arrangement is the
more important in as much as the wire has been
cut today.   I hope to keep the gunboat going as long
as you are at O'okiep and the wire is not
restored.

With best wishes, and the assurance
that I will do all in my power to assist you
                    I am,
                    Yours very faithfully,

                    A Milner

Page 2 of letter from Milner to Shelton

GARRISON OF OOKIEP RAISED JANUARY 1901

COLONEL SHELTON APPOINTED TO COMMAND GARRISON & TROOPS
JAN. 01

Capt Michell - Intelligence   Lt. Col. Shelton   Capt Gamble. Staff Officer.
Officer.   Commandant.

Namaqualand Field Force. ALL VOLUNTEERS EXCEPT BATTERY OF C.G.A. & 1ST Co C.T.

RAISED BY COLONEL SHELTON, D.S.O., FOR DEFENCE OF COPPER MINES — ON APPOINTMENT AS

SPECIAL SERVICE OFFICER TO HIS EXCELLENCY SIR ALFRED MILNER, GOVERNOR OF CAPE COLONY

Ookiep Garrison in line.

27

**GOVERNMENT HOUSE,
CAPE TOWN.**

February 8ᵏ, 1901.

The Governor and High Commissioner has received instructions from the Secretary of State for the Colonies to convey the thanks of

HIS MAJESTY THE KING

to the *Inhabitants of Namaqualand*

for their kind message of sympathy with him and the Royal Family in their great loss.

HIS MAJESTY is deeply touched by the many proofs of affection and loyalty which he has received from the Cape Colony and from all parts of South Africa.

*The Commandant,
Namaqualand
(O'okiep)*

Acknowledgement of message of sympathy

28

CHAPTER 2

MOBILE PATROLS

During the time Colonel Shelton was planning the defence of Namaqualand, General Smuts was instrumental in carrying out a complete re-organisation of the Boer Forces in Transvaal. Like General de Wet, he was a great strategist and had a clear and practical mind. He had established his force into four fighting units which were to advance towards the Cape Colony from different directions, north and south of the Orange River and then re-unite in the north-west area of the Cape. On this journey, the commandos were to recruit local Boer volunteers and rebel troops (rebels - the term used by the British for volunteers of different nationalities who fought with the Boers) who were eager to join the fight against the British.

Carrying the conflict into the British held territory, the object of the Boer attack was to disrupt the British Military system and Kitchener's lines of communication. In order to meet the threat by the Boer commandos, Shelton had raised two units of the Namaqualand Border Scouts. One was mounted consisting of two squadrons, a total of 436 men. The other was an Infantry Company, this had a strength of 200 men who were nearly all volunteers employed by the Cape Copper Company, and were being trained for the defence of the vitally important railway line from Port Nolloth to Okiep. This unit was formed and sworn in on January 10th, 1901. The officers appointed were Captain M. MacDonald, Lieutenant N.E. Moffat, who was traffic manager at Anenous, Lieutenants A.G. Meyrick, N. Dorrington and E. Hodge.

Knowing that General Smuts was determined to hit the British as hard as he possibly could, any time and anywhere, Kitchener increased his intelligence sources in order to cover every district throughout the vast theatre of guerrilla operations. These sources included many local intelligence agents who were situated in the remotest parts of the Cape. The first encounter Shelton's Border scouts had with the Boers was in the Bushmanland, to the east, on March 2nd, 1901, when a small party of commando raided Pella not far from the Orange River. Shelton's intelligence had reported about 200 Boers at Namies. Initially, Shelton lacked experienced scouts and was unable to take the offensive. He was also hampered by a lack of adequate water supplies for his troops. The Boers were holding the Bushmanland Waterholes and without them the scouts and mobile columns could not move. Shelton was forced to telegraph to his GHQ in Cape Town to suggest the enemy should be attacked from Kenhardt or Prieska and driven towards Okiep where he could engage them. Aggeneys, about thirty miles beyond Niep, where there was more water to be had, was also held by a small Boer commando unit. Shelton told his General it was vital that his part of the country should be cleared of the enemy as quickly as possible, the Boer activity was having a disastrous effect in the recruiting of more local men for Shelton's scouts. On hearing of the raid at Pella, and of the presence of the Boers at Namies and Aggeneys a number of would-be volunteers, about to join up, promptly bolted back to their homes in that area because they said they would not leave their families unprotected. About ninety men deserted Shelton for this reason, although many returned later to carry out their engagement, and eventually Shelton was able to build up his volunteer scouts to a reasonable strength.

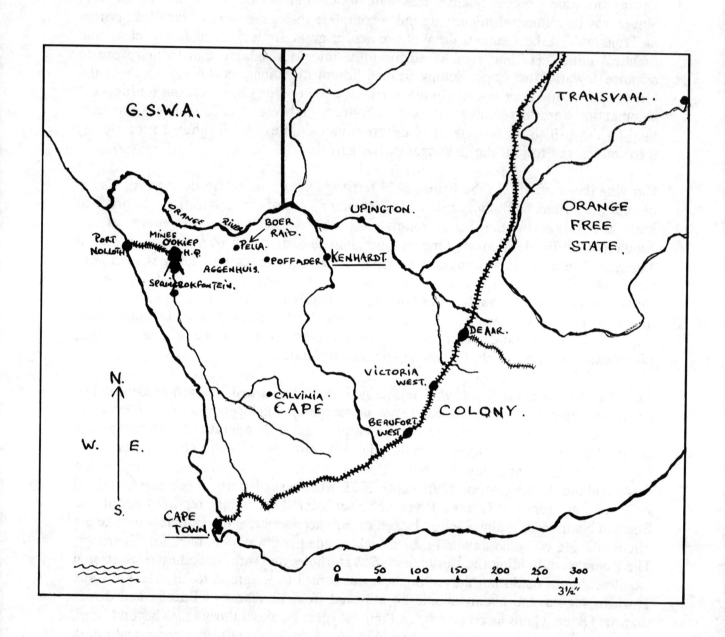

Boer raid on Pella - 2nd March 1901.

Some weeks later Shelton reported the Bushmanland field column now had 5 officers, 29 NCO's and 138 men including one Maxim machine gun. This would be operated by a small detachment of the Cape Garrison Artillery, and added greatly to the fire power of the column. He was then ordered to advance into Bushmanland and re-capture the waterholes at Aggeneys and other places, but British Intelligence had advised him that he should go via Amascon where the column could obtain necessary forage and some water. When the column finally reached Aggeneys the Boers had simply vanished into thin air - possibly back into German South-West Africa - a country which was still neutral, although the German High Command in Berlin were closely watching the situation. In order to keep a stricter check on the area, Shelton quickly established an outpost at Aggeneys which he placed under the command of Lieutenant Dixon (Namaqualand Border Scouts) who was to forward any intelligence to Shelton from eastern borders and generally monitor the movements of any commando he sighted. Scouting continued from April 1st 1901 around Pofadder area. Soon Dixon on the Orange River was able to tell Shelton he was watching two Boer farmers - George and John Lerm - with two other rebels - George and William Klindt - who had been hanging about Ramans Drift, and obtaining supplies from Le Rich and Company of Warmbad, German South-West Africa. Shelton also received intelligence from that particular area from Lieutenant Bowers of the NBS, who was obtaining further information on all Boer movement across the drift into the neutral state, from a German policeman, Sergeant

Ready for mobile patrol - 3rd Bn Queen's

31

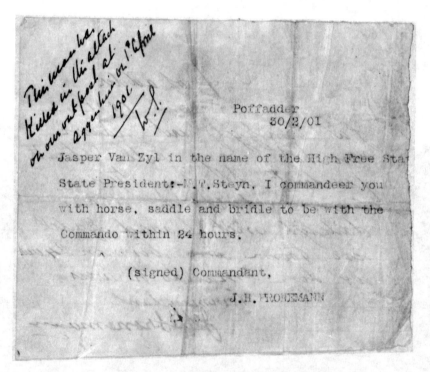

Original and translation of Commandeering Order to J van Zijl.
*See Shelton's endorsement - **This man was killed in the attack***
on our outpost at Aggenhuis on 1st April 1901

Krozier, who was in charge of Quarantine at Ramans Drift. Shelton had previously prohibited the export of foodstuffs to the firm of Le Rich and Company.

Further intelligence came from Lieutenant Dixon. He reported that a small guard of German troops, with thirty Hottentots, were patrolling the banks of the Orange River from Noam Drift up to Kakamas. Dixon had also located a large number of goats and horses at Zakol - between Schuit Drift and Kakamas Drift.

When Shelton's mobile column arrived at Pella he conferred with Lieutenants Dixon and Bowers and decided to leave twenty Border scouts with them and return to Okiep where information had been received of Boer commandos sighted south of Vanrhynsdorp. On the way back to Okiep the column was shadowed by Boer scouts and when it arrived at Aggeneys, Shelton decided to leave a further ten men at this out-post. When the British troops left this isolated post they were fired on by the Boer scouts who had watched them depart. In this skirmish two Boers were killed and three wounded. There were no casualties on the British side. On arrival in Okiep, Shelton organized a much stronger mounted infantry unit which he held ready for patrolling, but he had first to rest his men and their horses. The new column had a Maxim machine gun and a total strength of 174 officers and men. Hearing that the Boers had taken Aggeneys, Shelton decided to go back with the column.

Whilst Captain Montague was waiting for the reinforcements which Shelton was to bring, the Boers had dug in at Aggeneys, formerly held by his small Namaqualand Border Scout contingent. Montague was a highly experienced officer, but he realised he could not retake the Aggeneys outpost with the few Namaqualand Border Scouts he had with him. A man named Rich, serving with him, was also a local farmer who had some influence in the district and had many of his horses grazing about four miles to the west of the post, guarded by 12 men, when the Boers had swooped down on them, and stampeded and captured most of the horses.

Shelton had now heard that a Colonel Smith was operating in the North-West District and was approaching Kenhardt in order to drive any Boer commandos towards Shelton's column where they could be attacked. Shelton at once sent out scouts to meet Smith's men and when his column arrived at Aggeneys it was met by Captain Montague and went into a successful action against the enemy who retired from the British outpost. Aggeneys was re-occupied by Captain Montague's men on Saturday, April 6th, 1901 supported by troops from the new column. This important move re-opened the road to Pella where Shelton's troops would then be in striking distance of Namies. Shelton decided to advance to Pella. He ordered Montague to remain at Aggeneys and left him fresh supplies of food, forage, ammunition and more men. There was sufficient water in the waterholes at the re-taken post.

As Shelton advanced towards Pella his Intelligence Agent, Billy Cook, rode up to advise him that there had been a major move by Boer commando units in the southern area of his district, and that they had entered the Brandvlei and Calvinia area. On hearing this news Shelton knew that he had to contact Lieutenant Dixon as soon as possible and then return quickly to his Okiep headquarters. This he did, next day, having left some

Mr Billy Cook, one of Shelton's scouts departing on a mission

Okiep Copper Mines - Colonel Shelton's Head Quarters

reinforcements with Dixon. On April 15th, Shelton received more news of stronger Boer infiltration towards the Vanrhynsdorp area which prompted him to send an urgent message to his general in Cape Town requesting reinforcements. Shelton was still desperately short of experienced officers and hoped the authorities would realize this and accede to his request.

The German vessel **Gertrude Woerman**
by Courtesy of **Deutsche-Afrika Linien**

It was while Colonel Shelton was resting from his long journey to Pella, that he was given a strange telegram from the customs officials at Walfish Bay (GSWA) reporting that dead rats had been found in the cargo off-loaded at the port from a German steamer *Gertrude Woermann* and many had been thrown over board. Port and Health Officers at Port Nolloth considered this to be rather suspicious and immediately requested instructions from the British Commandant, "should the ship call at Port Nolloth on her way back to Cape Town?" Shelton replied with strict instructions that the ship should continue on her voyage and added that under no circumstances should communication be made with the vessel for the obvious risk of contracting any disease which rats could be carrying. Bubonic plague had broken out in Cape Town during March, 1901 and Shelton was taking no chances. He decided that precautionary and preventative measures had to be adopted. His only medical officer, Doctor Howard, in charge of all troops and civilians in Okiep and the entire district, was about to advise his C.O. to slaughter all pigs in the town of Okiep and neighbouring areas. No pigs were allowed

Cornish Copper miners - O'OKIEP - NAMAQUALAND 1901

to be kept in the town or environs. Gross violation or any disregard of the necessary order was to be severely dealt with under Martial Law. A prior consignment of pigs had arrived in Okiep via port Nolloth from the *Gertrude Woermann*.

Following this order Shelton was forced to impose some very strict regulations at Port Nolloth concerning the importation of fresh vegetables and fruit. Information had reached him that two local traders, Krapohl and Wrentmore, had managed to land a quantity of fruit and vegetables which had been duly destroyed by the authorities at the Port. Although these regulations created much hardship for certain traders, especially those who sold to Germans in GSWA, it resulted in keeping Bubonic plague out of Namaqualand.

As Shelton continued to receive much intelligence from various sources indicating the Boers were on the move towards his district he called his officers together to review the general situation of defence which had been arranged. Unknown to him one of his staff had written a humorous little ditty which he had dedicated to his CO and at the meeting this was duly presented to him. On reading the text, Shelton was very pleased to accept the comic verse, and was so impressed that he read it out to all his officers and men. This was met by much laughter and approval by the entire garrison. Shelton took a copy of it and then sent the original to his daughter in England, adding some translation on the bottom. This is a unique piece of Okiep history from the British Commandant during troubled times in the North-West Cape Colony.

Okiep Copper Mines - Colonel Shelton's Head Quarters

A TOWN GUARD DITTY

1. We've left out peaceful offices, our mines and smelting works
    We're learning how to shoulder arms & down with him who shirks,
    And when the Hooter's blast is heard like bees around we swarm,
    For if our brother Boer should come we hope to make him warm.

    (Chorus) For it's form fours, left wheel, where are you going now,
    And it's quick march, right form, half of
    'em don't know how
    And it's Blackwatch, hardloep, footsac to the right,
    And three cheers for the Commandant but never a Boer in sight.

2. There's the Major with the Captain, just see their martial tread
    and there's the heaven born Adjutant, who never goes to bed,
    Lieutenants here, & sergeants there, & privates by the score,
    And nominal rolls, Heaven rest our souls, but never a blooming Boer.
    For it's form fours &c &c

3. We march upon the copper heaps, we lay upon the stones,
    We grovel in the skimpings, may Heaven rest our bones,
    We drill by day, and in our dreams we hear the Hooter's roar,
    Our clothes are bursting at the seams but never a blooming Boer.
    For it's form fours &c &c.

4. Sure we're making forts and piling bags as cheerful as can be,
    The barbed wire tears our clothes to rags, but Briton's shall be free,
    The Colonel on his prancing steed doth groan to hear the band
    But we never heed the music as we march upon the sand.
    For it's form fours &c &c

5. Oh war it may be glory, and fighting may be fun,
    But that's another story when the shooting has begun,

A TOWN GUARD DITTY.

-:-:-:-:-:-:-

1. We've left out peaceful offices, our mines and smelting works
   We're learning how to shoulder arms & down with him who shirks,
   And when the Hooter's blast is heard like bees around we swarm,
   For if our brother Boer should come we hope to make him warm.

   (Chorus) For its form fours, left wheel, where are you going now,
   And it's quick march, right form, half of 'em dont know how
   And it's Blackwatch, hardloep, footsac to the right,
   And three cheers for the Commandant but never a Boer in
   sight.

2. There's the Major with the Captain, just see their martial tread
   And there's the heaven born Adjutant, who never goes to bed,
   Lieutenants here, & sergeants there, & privates by the score,
   And nominal rolls, Heaven rest our souls, but never a blooming Boer.
   For it's form fours &c &c.

3. We march upon the copper heaps, we lay upon the stones,
   We grovel in the skimpings, may Heaven rest our bones,
   We drill by day, and in our dreams we hear the Hooter's roar,
   Our clothes are bursting at the seams but never a blooming Boer.
   For it's form fours &c &c.

4. Sure were making forts and piling bags as cheerful as can be,
   The barbed wire tears our clothes to rags, but Briton's shall befree
   The Colonel on his prancing steed doth groan to hear the Band
   But we never heed the music as we march upon the sand.
   For it's form fours &c &c.

5. Oh war it may be glory, and fighting may be fun,
   But that's another story when the shooting has begun,
   So now we're doing mark time, so now we're forming fours,
   And now we bless the Colonel, and now we cuss the Boers.
   For it's form fours &c &c.

-:-:-:-:-:-:-:-:-:-:-
-:-:-:-:-:-:-
-:-:-

Dedicated to Lieut.Colonel Shelton, D.A.A.G.
Commandant,
NAMAQUALAND.
by the Author.

O'okiep,
February, 1901.

39

The Town Guard Ditty, showing Shelton's translations for his daughter
(Note: Shelton says "I have 13 miles of barbed wire around the town")

So now we're doing mark time, so now we've forming fours.
And now we bless the Colonel, and now we cuss the Boers.
For it's form fours &c &c

Dedicated to Lieut, Colonel Shelton, D.A.A.G.
Commandant,
NAMAQUALAND.

by the Author.

O'okiep,
February, 1901

By May 1901, the fortunes of war were beginning to turn against the Boers with the situation becoming more gloomy for them. It was decided to endeavour to reach some satisfactory agreement with the British and to this end General Smuts contacted President Kruger who was miles away in exile in Utrecht. Unfortunately, the old ex-President, who was completely out of touch with the general situation, ordered Smuts to continue the fight to the 'bitter end' if necessary. Following these instructions Smuts made further plans to infiltrate deeper into the Cape Colony, although this manoeuvre was to cost the lives of half of his men, it was regarded by the British as one of the greatest feats of the entire war.

Shelton's intelligence agents who were operating along the Orange River in the Ramans Drift area had intercepted some letters suspected of containing information useful to the Boers. When they had been forwarded to the British Commandant and steamed open it was discovered that one of them was a communication from one Huiligard B Steyn, indicating that Boer sympathizers were operating in GSWA. It was immediately sent to Colonel Shelton who ordered that a copy be taken of it and the original sent on through normal channels if possible.

As Smuts began his incursion into the North-West Cape, the British Army patrols were preparing to meet the threat to the British owned Colony which had, up to now, been little affected by the war and had virtually no scorched terrain, but was now to become a theatre of intensive guerrilla operations. The thirteen blockhouses which had been strategically placed around Okiep were manned by members of the Okiep Town Guard, the 1st Battalion of the Namaqualand Border Scouts and the 3rd Battalion of the Queen's Royal West Surrey Regiment.

With thirteen miles of barbed wire placed along the out and inner defences, Okiep was now a fortified town and was ready to meet the invasion of the commando units who were shortly to arrive in the area. Colonel Shelton was not content to sit and wait for the Boers and was eager to leave with a large mobile patrol to reconnoitre the southern area as far as Garies. The Town Guards at the neighbouring copper mining settlements of Concordia and Nababeep had been partially trained by the NCO's of Shelton's company which could give protection in the event of attack by small Boer units. With the advance of General Smuts' commandos these Boer units were beginning to swell in numbers as local volunteers joined them. As the commandos increased in strength,

(COPY)

Kakamas, 30-4-01.

My Own fondest Darling:-

    Can you ever believe that I am writing to you from this place? The last letter I wrote you was from the Aberdeen District, and this one from the world's end. We came to assist the Kenhardt Burghers, as well as the Calvinia Burghers, so we took the opportunity to come to the German Territory so as to get some letters and important reports through to Europe, as well as to _you_. Oh! My Darling, you can never imagine what a treat it is again to give vent to my feelings. My previous letters were merley to let you know that I was still in good health. I can never tell you how I am longing for you; but what on earth is the good of longing, when it is impossible to meet. Anyhow I hope we shall some day be together again, and make up for all the lost time, not so, Sweetest?

    Ja mijn Kind, since last we were together, I have gone through many narrow paths, and am daily going through them; God has helped me thus far and I am positive He will protect me further. I hope Dearest, that you wont worry about me, always be cheerful - alles zal recht komen.

    I have heaps to tell you, but will wait until we meet, which I hope wont be long. How is dear old Lente? Kindly give her my best love, also to the other girls and your dear Mother.

                With heaps of love and fondest kisses,

                  Your own and only,

                    (Sgnd.) Hulligard(?)

P.S. I shall be glad to hear from you at an early date. Please address "Huligard B.Steyn on one envelope and place it in another and address it to D.N.Liebenberg, Schuit Drift P.K. Warmbad xxxt. Duitsch Zuid West Africa. I have arranged further; so I am sure they will reach their proper destination.

                Heaps of love,

                  Yours, (H.S.)

J.

Copy of letter from Huligard B. Steyn

41

COLONIAL DEFENCE FORCE.

O'OKIEP TOWN GUARD.

OATH OF ALLEGIANCE.

I, *Wm Isaac*

of *O'O Kief Namaqualand*

do sincerely promise that I will be faithful and bear true allegiance
to Her Majesty Queen Victoria as lawful Sovereign of the United
Kingdom of Great Britain and Ireland, and of the Colony of the Cape
of Good Hope, and to Her Heirs and Successors according to Law.

Declared this *21*

day of *Jany* 1901. *William Isaac*

Before me, *to Shelton Lt Colonel*

Military Commandant, *& A.A.G.*

Namaqualand.

at *O'Okiep* this *21* day of *Jany* 1901.

*As the local volunteers joined the Town Guards they were required to
declare an **Oath of Allegiance** to H.M. Queen Victoria*

Envelope containing intelligence to Col. Shelton from his agent
at Ramans Drift G.S.W.A.

General Smuts realised that he would be in a much stronger position to negotiate better terms with the British when the final conflict was eventually over.

During the slow advance to the Cape, Smuts and his commandos ran into severe weather conditions. Furthermore their boots had worn out, their clothing was torn and tattered, some even wearing grain bags hastily adapted to protect themselves from the elements. A few had managed to obtain some British uniforms, not knowing of Kitchener's proclamation that any enemy so dressed would be shot immediately. They were tired, cold and hungry and their horses near to exhaustion. General Smuts ordered his men to rest. It was time to take stock of his fighting force. Clothes, ammunition, food and fresh horses were urgently needed. Smuts, an able strategist, was already formulating a plan of attack in the far off North-West Cape, and with his men refreshed and properly fed, he was determined to give the British a lot of trouble.

On August 9th, 1901, Shelton again urgently requested reinforcements with much emphasis on mounted infantry. The military authorities at GHQ had already considered his difficult position and had arranged for an officer of the Royal Artillery to join him at his headquarters. This was Colonel White who had a great deal of experience with mounted columns, especially when field guns were deployed. He was going to be of the greatest help to Shelton who needed all the officers he could get.

As soon as White arrived in Okiep Shelton explained the general situation and it was agreed that White should take out another field column immediately to patrol the north-eastern area of the Orange River. Much activity had been reported from that area and it would be an opportunity for supplies to be taken by the column to the small detachments Shelton had previously left at Aggeneys, Pella and Namies. He had already ordered his small force of 70 men from Alewynsfontein to re-inforce those at the Pella out-station. Colonel White's column made good progress as they entered the

3rd Queen's loading mule for mobile patrol

44

inhospitable country around Aggeneys.

This operation left the whole of the south-western borders practically undefended as Shelton had only twenty Namaqualand Border Scouts at Garies under the command of Lieutenant Dixon. This officer, who had now returned to Okiep was immediately sent back to the southern area in order to report any Boer movements from the Garies area. The only other post Shelton had was at Ramans Drift on the Orange River where twenty-five NCO's and men of the NBS were still under the command of Lieutenant Bowers. At 9am on August 9th, intelligence reached Shelton that telegraphic communication with Cape Town had been cut. At 5pm the same day the Deputy Officer at Garies informed him that the 'Post Cart' which had left for Cape Town with mail had returned with information that the Boers had entered the town of Vanrhynsdorp in a considerable force. The mail cart actually arrived back at Garies at 3pm when the driver reported that on nearing Vanrhynsdorp he had met a messenger sent out by the Postmaster there to warn him of the immediate danger and to advise him to return to Garies, as there were seventy Boers in the town under the command of Steenkamp. The commando had entered Vanrhynsdorp after shooting up a British Camp killing two men and all the horses, as well as creating much trouble and havoc.

Until land communications had been restored Shelton's only means of communicating with the outside world was via Port Nolloth and the sea to Cape Town. This was a slow process compared with the telegraph. Shelton decided to send all future messages by sea to Cape Town. On hearing this unwelcome news Shelton sent an urgent message to HQ in Cape Town via Port Nolloth stating that he was now dependent on his Town Guards for the defence or Okiep and the valuable copper mines. He had to consider how best he could deploy the men under his command - it was a difficult task.

Two local rebel prisoners captured at Nous by Colonel White

45

In late August, intelligence sources operating with Colonel White's mobile column in the north-eastern area of the Orange River reported that many Boer families and others had trekked via Schuit Drift into the neutral German Territory from Pofadder and the Kenhardt district, taking with them much stock of all kinds. These families were living on farms between Schuit Drift, Noems Drift and Ramans Drift on the German side. One such farm had been leased by the German government to about ten Boer Families who were paying rent of seventeen pounds ten shillings a year. Other families were reported to have occupied similar farms at Jerusalem, Blydeverwachte, Ouder Maathie, Gwendoorn, Odabis and Vetoer. There were many rebels among them but all the families were short of bread and general provisions. The German authorities had also levied a 'wheel tax' of two pounds for each wagon entering their territory which had amounted to £400. Every family also had to pay £7 10s when settling in the neutral state. On the Orange River the small garrison of twenty German soldiers were stationed at Schuit Drift and this had already been reported to Colonel Shelton by Lieutenant Bowers, who was still obtaining information on their everyday movements.

All loaded up with Maxim machine gun for mobile patrol - Namaqualand 1901

As all exports and imports of foodstuffs had been restricted by Colonel Shelton it was necessary to keep a strict watch on traders and any Boer families who were endeavouring to bring provisions into Namaqualand. Meanwhile, Colonel White's column was also gathering in all horses, mules, oxen and sheep that they could find throughout the area. White sent Shelton a report from Nous saying "the country is clear of the enemy am sweeping all stock in here to go forward towards you and already have some 10,000 in hand. The owners of which are for the most part accompanying their property. I go on the 25th August to Schuit Drift to meet Lieutenant Bowers and then sweep the country along the river westward and if reports are correct shall probably get 10,000 to 15,000 head more stock. It will probably be hopeless to send all this in to Kaitob as there will not be sufficient water. Will you consider the possibility of holding Aggeneys and Rozynbosch in which case the sheep at least could be left there? As far as I can see I shall be back at Pofadder about the 30th (August) - Pella the 31st or 1st and movements after that will depend on forward situation of stock and how you propose to dispose of it. I will also return with the troops who will revert to your command as soon as active operations cease." Signed Col White.

Captain Williams on mobile patrol, North Eastern Area

Colonel Shelton with fellow officers 3rd Queen's Royal West Surrey Regiment, Namaqualand Field Force.

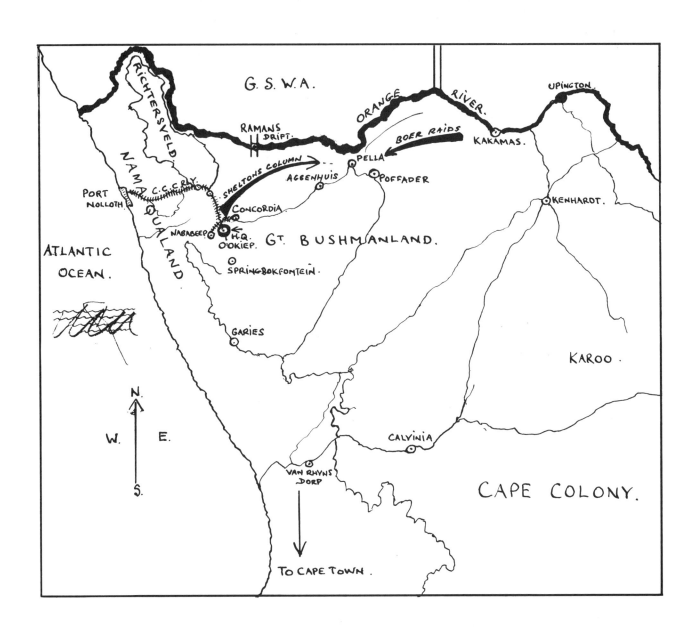

Map of North Western Cape Colony showing Okiep and Shelton's Mobile Columns as well as direction of Boer raids.

49

When Shelton received White's message he organized a detachment under Captain Williams to report to Aggeneys and guard the post there. Williams took two other officers with him and a hundred men with one Maxim machine gun. Shelton also sent a further thirty-five men to Kaitob to protect the large quantity of stock which Colonel White had gathered. These animals were grazing there, but owing to a severe drought were dying at the rate of a few hundred per week. Shelton was now in a position where he had large supplies and forage situated throughout his north-eastern area. However, on the southern areas from Okiep there was more evidence of intense Boer activity near Garies.

CHAPTER 3

SKIRMISHING WITH BROTHER BOER

It was now well over two weeks since Shelton had received any mail either by land or sea. The Post cart which normally brought the mail was unable to move south from Garies and the supply ship *SS Nautilus* was not due at Port Nolloth until the end of the month, bringing additional mail and welcome supplies for Shelton's garrison and field force. Word was again received in Okiep that the telegraph line had been cut between Garies and Vanrhynsdorp. The Boers were certainly on their way with strength unknown and it was now becoming obvious the commando units had penetrated well into the Cape Colony. The British Field Intelligence Department was having some difficulty in monitoring their progress and the job of communication over such a vast area was made harder when telegraph wires were cut and the only other method of land communication was the horse. Sometimes the messages got through to their destination and on other occasions they simply disappeared. Colonel Shelton acted swiftly. He ordered Lieutenant Dixon to investigate the area surrounding Garies and on the 7th September 1901 Dixon took a patrol of fifteen men on this mission. While he was away a Boer patrol circled round him and on the 11th had ridden into Garies where they were immediately engaged by the few Namaqualand Border Scouts remaining behind to protect the town. The Boers had now completely cut Garies off and had destroyed the telegraph wires leading to Okiep. Hopelessly out-numbered, the few scouts were soon taken prisoner despite putting up fierce resistance. The Boers took their horses and their rifles and ammunition but did not take them prisoner. They also entered the post office and burnt all the mail and documents they found.

Lieutenant Dixon having sighted a strong enemy commando sent a scout back to Okiep to ask for reinforcements to be sent immediately to Garies. This man was lucky enough to arrive safely at the British Headquarters, whereupon Shelton quickly organized a strong mounted detachment of NBS consisting of two officers and fifty men with one Maxim machine gun. The column left immediately to join Dixon just north of Garies which the Boers still held. Meanwhile Colonel White's mobile field column, which had been operating north-east of Okiep in Bushmanland, had returned to the headquarters at Okiep on the 6th September, with little or no water left. As White was now back and his term of service had expired he waited for a ship to take him from Port Nolloth back to Cape Town, but at the same time he had offered to act for Shelton during the Commandant's absence.

In order to back up the mobile patrol which had already left for Garies, Shelton had decided to take a further patrol and join Lieutenant Dixon in the Garies district. He was grateful for the extra help he was receiving from White and this enabled him to act more swiftly and seek the Boer commando which had penetrated his district. Shelton's column consisted of nine officers and 150 men all mounted. He had decided to go via Bowesdorp and if the Boers had managed to take Garies, he would then engage them and attempt to drive them out. After that the repair of the telegraph lines was essential, as was the re-establishment of the post cart service.

Early on the morning of the 13th September the column left with advance scouts well ahead to reconnoitre the area towards Bowesdorp which was located 53 miles south of Okiep. Shelton's column was widely dispersed with every man diligently watching the surrounding terrain for any sign or movement which might indicate an ambush. However, on this short venture no attack came and the column reached Bowesdorp

A group of 3rd Queen's waiting for a Boer Commando

safely the same evening. Here they halted for a necessary rest. Shelton then concentrated his force to press on to Garies, leaving a further small detachment under one officer with 20 men to defend the stores and forage at Bowesdorp. As the main force of Shelton's column advanced, a scout raced up to tell him that the enemy had already occupied Garies. The scout said that intelligence had come via the Mission Station at Leliefontein indicating a strong Boer commando was at Daamsland, south of the mission. The scout also reported that farmers had seen about 250 Boers with some 700 horses at Doornkraal 18 miles south-east of Garies. The commando was sending out advance scouts to east and west of this area to look for and bring in horses and supplies, and at the same time recruit as many young men as possible to fight with them. Lieutenant Dixon, who should have been in Garies, when the Boer commando entered, was away on patrol (as has already been mentioned) and, realizing his force was too small to intervene, he made a detour and joined Shelton's main column, just north of the town. The additional information from Dixon was of the greatest importance to his CO. Shelton sent word down the column to prepare for immediate action as they were now virtually on top of the enemy. Actually, his column had already been spotted by a Boer look-out, who swiftly passed the news back to his general - S.G. Maritz - who on hearing this unwelcome information began to leave the town, not wishing to engage the British patrol. Their departure was really of no consequence to the Boers as they had managed to obtain some food and clothing from various stores in the town. Soon General Maritz and his men were to re-unite with the main force under General Smuts. More commandos were advancing into the Cape daily, and although scattered were becoming a strong and formidable force. When Colonel Shelton entered Garies, the enemy had completely vanished into the open country, although they had left their mark. The Post Office had been entered and certain stores in the town had been looted, one of which belonged to Philip Rosenberg, a merchant who had lost boots and clothing. The value amounted to £214.14s. For these articles the Boers left commandeered receipts signed 'Maritz T.V.K. 13/9.01 P.V.D. Nerme', 'Maritz T.V.K. Sergeant E de B Spinger O.V.S.'. The store of Gerard Genis was looted of goods to the value of £500.16s and similar notes were left in this case. H. Schapera, merchant, suffered also, with the Boers pulling up the floor in his shop. Provisions amounted to £14.18s being taken. In Doornkraal the store of Max Abel was looted to the value of £70. About 15 horse were taken by the Boers from the town and some more from farmers. At Eyzelsfontein Endoorn, Kraairivier, Leliefontein more horses were taken.

While Colonel Shelton was reviewing the situation at Garies, he learned of a brave act by an old member of his Namaqualand Border Scouts, one Barnabas Links, who was 60 years of age and was one of the 5 scouts left in Garies by Lieutenant Dixon. Links had been ordered by Dixon to inspect and if necessary repair the telegraph line near Garies. On seeing the Boers entering the town, he took cover in a koppie which commanded the town. He immediately opened fire on the enemy and kept shooting until his ammunition was exhausted. He was then surrounded and made prisoner. The Boers took him back to the local jail threatened to 'sjambok' (pronounced shambok - meaning beat) him and

Ready for Mobile Patrol. Officers and men 3rd Queen's, Namagualand Field Force.

burnt all his belongings, taking away his horse and rifle. Shelton considered the brave act deserved a reward and sanctioned a free issue of kit to Links to replace what had been taken by the Boers. This delighted the old man immensely. On the other hand Shelton convened a Court of Enquiry at Garies to investigate and report upon the full circumstances of the surrender of the five scouts.

The volunteers who joined the Boers were termed by the British as rebels and quite a few came from Vanrhynsdorp and Garies area. A complete list of their names was given to Colonel Shelton by British Field Intelligence Officer James Caldow, on September 27th, 1901 and if any had been taken prisoner they would have been shot.

Colonel Shelton had not engaged the elusive Boers this time but they were re-grouping fast and intelligence had indicated they were moving northwards rapidly. Shelton decided to return to Okiep where he could take stock of the situation and send a full report to his general in Cape Town.

*Piece of burnt mail from Garies Post Office. (Shelton has written on it **Burnt by enemy in Garies Post Office Sept, 11th 1901**)*

He left the defence of Garies under Lieutenant Hodge with 50 men until such time he could despatch a stronger force. When he arrived back at Okiep he immediately called a meeting of senior officers which included Colonel White in order to review the now serious situation. Shelton knew it was necessary to ask White to take out another mobile column this time to Garies and further south to operate on the southern border of the district.

On October 1st, 1901, Colonel White RA, took the field column out once again to explore the lower part of Namaqualand for Boer activity. Shelton sent a message to General French at Middelburg:

"A field column under the command of Lieutenant Col White RA left O'OKiep HQ on October 1st to operate on the southern borders of my district. Leaving a detachment at Garies, strength one officer and 70 men, Colonel White moved on night of 5th to Dikdoorn 18 miles south of Garies and pushed to Varskop, 22 miles south along main road, reporting all clear. Telegraph lines very badly damaged. On 6th White reported from Bitterfontein 40 spies south-south-east of Garies. Said about 300 enemy of whom 100 unarmed passed across road from west to east about 20 miles south on 3rd inst. He intended moving south by Varsbrach and Klipkraal. He reports 30 poles, 50 insulators and 5 coils of wire required to repair telegraph line so far. Can you send these? White reported from Klipkraal on 7th October - 15 miles north of Olifants River 'all clear' but found sites of Boer camps. On 2nd October 200 Boers with 700 horses had evidently crossed river at Ebenezer and then advanced to Clanwilliam. White was moving to Ebenezer to check and then patrol Clanwilliam if threatened. He says he has picked up several rebel horses left behind. This is the last I have heard of him. He reports plenty of supplies in country he is moving through and I am keeping him well supplied at Garies." --- signed Shelton.

3rd Bn Queen's Maxim machine gun. Namaqualand Field Force

Men of the 3rd Bn of the Queen's at bayonet practice.

3rd Queen's removing wounded

On October 15th, after Shelton's message to French, Colonel White also reported to the general, sending a copy to Shelton for information. His text is as follows:

"Garies. My column was concentrated here by the 4th October, leaving a strong post and I moved on 5th with about 250 men and Maxim, with a view to clearing the southern borders of Namaqualand district. As I proceeded southward I came across tracks of several bodies of the enemy, amounting in the aggregate to 700 or 800 men together with about 700 remounts they had collected in the Calvinia and Van Rhyns Dorp districts. All information pointed to their moving on Clanwilliam. To make sure of the safety of that place I pushed on through the Zandveldt to Ebenezer near the mouth of the Olifants River (8th Oct, 1901) and then moved rapidly on Van Rhyns Dorp (morning of 9th) as I heard of a body of enemy near there. There were only 3 hostile scouts on the heights near the town who galloped off on our approach. The party reported had been 100 strong of whom only 30 were armed, and with Cape carts full of wounded. This party had moved off through Van Rhyns Dorp towards Calvinia. At Van Rhyns Dorp I received a despatch from the officer commanding the south-west district at Clanwilliam in reply to a note sent by me from Garies on the 5th Oct. He assured me of his security and that the main body of enemy had passed to south of him further than I could follow with the Namaqualand Field Force without the sanction of the GOC as it would leave this very large district quite denuded of mobile troops. I decided to return to Garies by unfrequented roads to the east of the main road, so as to thoroughly search the country. I arrived at Garies on 14th October (1901). I have driven in as much rebel stock as I require for use, and have ordered the remainder to be collected at specified places. I shall arrange with O/C Namaqualand (Colonel Shelton) as to disposal of these. Meanwhile I retain the receipts until the proper owners call upon me in person for them (the receipts left by raiding Boers in the stores and post office in Garies). Almost without exception, the youths of Van Rhyns Dorp district have joined the rebels. After the mild experiences which followed their efforts of last year still seem to regard 'rebellion' as an agreeable recreation, to be followed perhaps by the withdrawal of a vote which some of them do not possess. The older people, who have remained at home, will give no information (except to the enemy) and are as a whole, distinctly hostile. I have treated them as such. There have been but few additions to the rebel forces from the mining districts of Namaqualand where the population is mostly English or of English extraction. The Van Rhyns Dorp district requires very severe treatment and I suggest the imposition of very heavy fines for damages to telegraph lines and for compensation to local storekeepers who are mostly local Jews and who have lost severely by the action of local banditti. I strongly advocate a series of **executions** of local rebels, when captured, on the scene of their crimes. After the resting of our horses and refitting, I propose to move from here towards Calvinia and thence towards Clanwilliam. This should clear the Bokkeveld country and at least

3rd Bn. The Queen's - sword drill.

59

On mobile patrol near Pella

The Mascot Lamb of the 3rd Bn Queen's.
Colonel Shelton with colleague outside his H.Q. Office

60

will make a display of force, which may influence those that have not yet joined the rebels. I shall be glad to receive as soon as possible some idea of the general plan of action in the western provinces, so as to regulate my movements accordingly. The health of the troops has been very good and the column has covered 297 miles in the 13 marching days since it left O'Okiep. The horses therefore want a few days rest. I shall meet O/C Namaqualand before sending this and will ask him to note his views hereon. Bowesdorp October 16th, 1901."

White continues his letter -

"I have met Colonel Shelton here today and we agree that the movement to Pella of 30 rebels can be met by the detachment at Aggeneys which number about 70." --- signed W.L. White Lieutenant Col Namaqualand Field Force.

Colonel Shelton then added a short postscript:

"Notes by O/C Namaqualand --- In concurrence with Colonel White's desire I add the following notes. Any rebels that may be in my district are to be found on the V.R. Dorp border which is a hot bed of rebels and seditious. I strongly endorse and support Colonel White's suggestions as to the most drastic measures being necessary to reduce that district to a proper spirit of subordination. I am in perfect accord with Colonel White as to the future movements of the NFF but I take this opportunity in view of the activity of the enemy in this neighbourhood to strongly advocate and advise the strengthening of the garrison of this district. I feel convinced that sooner or later the rebels will be driven in this direction and we shall find Namaqualand the theatre of very lively operations. Rebel stock. It is difficult to find food and water for this stock. To obviate this I will as opportunity offers sell the stock to loyal farmers and others at nominal prices."--- signed Lieutenant Col W. Shelton, Commanding District O'Okiep 17 October 1901. Forwarded by German steamer from Port Nolloth 18th October 1901.

Shelton later drafted another letter to his general in Cape Town. It was now 25th November, 1901. This letter reads:

"The necessity for providing against the possibility of a siege of the copper mining area and my HQ is now of paramount importance. Our land communication with the outer world has been **entirely severed** since August last and we have since then been dependent on the sea for our supplies. The failure of crops, owing to drought, necessitates the greatest economy. The foodstuffs can be obtained at any time by accredited German traders on permits. The danger here is that the enemy has been unusually active all along the Orange River particularly at Schuit Drift, and any convoys of supplies going into German territory by either Ramans Drift or Schuit Drift run a great risk of being attacked and captured. One such wagon fully loaded with supplies was captured by the enemy between

61

3rd Queen's completing their ablutions. Blockhouse in background, left.

Okiep and Pella last week. 86 head of cattle were taken. It is impossible to protect all these supply columns. My orders are clear; to adopt every measure to prevent supplies and horses falling into the hands of the enemy. So far I have been successful except in one or two minor cases. I shall be glad to receive any reinforcements you may be able to send me etc."--- signed W. Shelton. Sent by *SS Nautilus* sailing Port Nolloth 25th November, 1901.

Letter from Shelton's Intelligence agent in G.S.W.A.

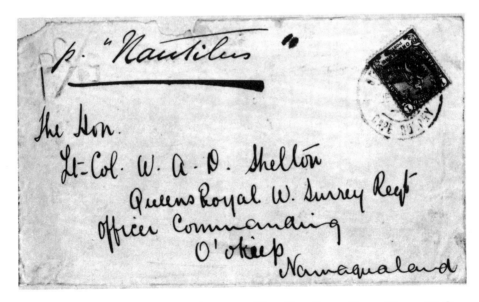

Envelope conveyed to Shelton via Nautilus from Cape Town H.Q.

CHAPTER 4

THE BOERS ADVANCE

Colonel Shelton's orders to stop all foodstuffs being imported into Namaqualand were followed by a similar regulation to check the export of food into German South-West Africa. British Intelligence, who were closely watching the Orange River area of Ramans Drift and Schuit Drift, had firm evidence that large amounts of supplies were finding their way into Boer hands at Kakamas and Kenhardt. Le Riche and Company were supplying rebels and Boer refugees with grain and food from Namaqualand, much of which was being passed on to commando units. Shelton, anxious this should cease, sent a notice of the export prohibition to all German storekeepers in his district. This embargo caused much hardship for the traders, who were keen to transact business on both sides of the river. Shelton had considered this situation very carefully and decided to issue permits to selected traders so that he could exercise strict control.

While Colonel Shelton was busy with these administrative matters he was asked to take evidence involving a serious incident which had occurred within his own garrison. Evidently, Captain Gamble (who, it will be recalled, had been specially selected and appointed by His Excellency, Lord Milner, to assist Shelton and was commanding the Namaqualand Border Scouts) had been involved in a fight with Lieutenant Cawston of the same company. It appears that this happened on December 4th in the dining room of the boarding house in which Lieutenant Cawston had permission from Shelton to take

3rd Bn Queen's engaging Boers on the
open veld

his meals since there was no Mess. As a consequence of the assault committed by Captain Gamble upon Cawston, both officers were placed under open arrest and the evidence was forwarded to General Settle in Cape Town with Shelton's recommendations: "The commission of so grave an offence renders Captain Gamble liable for trial by General Court Martial on a charge of 'Conduct unbecoming an officer and gentleman etc.,and as the court could not but find him guilty he must infallibly be cashiered. Captain Gamble was appointed to my staff by HE Lord Milner in January last, and to a commission in the SAIMF. He gave me most valuable assistance in raising the Namaqualand Border Scouts and as I could obtain no regular officers for the Corps, I appointed him, with the approval of the G.O.C., to the command of the Corps. From that time to the present he has been indefatigable in his work and endeavours to bring his Corps to a condition of efficiency, and in the deplorable circumstances which I now report I am most anxious to spare him such a terrible disgrace, which would seriously damage his civil career, but the display of such ungovernable temper, even under such provocation as is testified by Captain Shaw and Lieutenant Nethersole, and actuated by intense personal dislike, clearly shows that Capt Gamble is not fitted to be in command of men. I have the honour therefore to request that Captain Gamble may be allowed to resign his commission. Captain Gamble remains under open arrest pending decision of GOC and I have appointed Captain Montague to temporary command of NBS. I wish to add that Captain Gamble, in acceding to the request of HE the Governor, to volunteer for temporary service in Namaqualand, gave up a very lucrative employment. He had no previous military experience (and this applies to **all** the officers of the NBS except Captain Montague) but had previously been employed in the PWD as assistant architect for three or four years." The three officers who were present on the occasion

The ambulance of the 3rd Bn Queen's

of the assault and submitted evidence were; Capt Freeland RA Senior Officer, Capt Shaw 3rd Queens and Lieutenant Nethersole CGA.

Colonel Shelton's request was subsequently approved by the GOC (General French) and Capt Montague's appointment was confirmed.

The Namaqualand Border Scouts had now a fighting force of 420 men with 9 officers. Not one of these volunteers belonged to the regular army, in fact most of them were local farmers. Two of their subalterns were promoted from the ranks of the Cape Town Highlanders. This Corps had neither Paymaster nor Quartermaster. The pay for these men presented problems because they were deployed in several small detachments which operated extensively over his vast district. Travel was extremely difficult owing to the absence of railways and good road. Nevertheless, Colonel Shelton made sure that he received enough money for them from military authorities in Cape Town. The average amount of money to be found for the NBS each month was between £3,000 and £4,000. Shelton's 'Imprest' account running at times at as much as £7,000 to £8,000 monthly. This amount was exclusive of payment to all the Town Guards. He was responsible for a great deal of administration in addition to his main task, the defence of Namaqualand.

*Colonel Shelton on **Jacksnipe** about to leave on mobile patrol
to Aggeneys*

Handing out of the "smokes". Sergeants of the 3rd Bn. of the Queen's at O'OKiep.

In December 1901 the Boers were concentrating fast in the south-west Cape. General Smuts had linked up with Generals J.L. Van Deventer and S.G. Maritz, and was already planning a sortie to the far off town of Kakamas situated on the Orange River, a long and dangerous journey through strong British military patrols. Smuts was well aware of the rigours of this journey. On arrival at Kakamas he was to organise a large commando unit in the area. Again the British Field Intelligence was monitoring all Boer Movement towards the Orange River and advised Shelton accordingly. While Smuts was away General Ben Bouwer was reported to be in charge of the main commando force. As Shelton received the news of this latest move by his enemy, he became worried about the rapid incursion being made by Smuts into his district and sent an urgent message to his General in Cape Town:

"With reference to my recent telegram of December 19th and the movement of the whole of my Field Force as Colonel White's field column to Schuit Drift and Kakemas, the very large district under my command is practically denuded of mobile troops and the defence of the valuable copper mines at O'Okiep, Concordia and Nababeep, the railway, Cape Copper Company Workshops, locomotives and rolling stock, slip way and jetty etc., at Port Nolloth is now entirely dependent upon the district Town Guard Battalion. In view of the proximity of the enemy both on my southern and eastern borders and the great value of the property in this district, for which I am responsible, I wish to bring the following points to your notice for urgent attention. The small mobile force originally sent to Namaqualand for the protection of property in the neighbourhood of the copper mines comprised 50 men of the CGA and 100 of CTH. On my assuming command of the district, and our land communications being cut, a gunboat was sent to Port Nolloth, and accordingly the detachment of CGA and CTH were reinforced. I received authority to organise local Town Guards and raise a corps of Mounted Scouts to the number of 100. Later, I obtained permission to increase this corps to 100 of all ranks and to form a Mounted Infantry Company supported by two field guns and a Galloping Maxim sent from Cape Town. I fortified O'Okiep and Port Nolloth and at the latter place had the assistance of 2 machine guns and gun detachment with an officer landed from *HMS Magpie* (Lieutenant Laird RN). By April 1st I had a small and fairly efficient mobile force of about 100 Mounted Infantry (drawn from CGA and CTH). About 420 NBS (mounted) with two 9 lb field guns and 2 Maxims. Despite the several attempts to invade the district since the Pella raid of March last, I succeeded so far in keeping my district clear of the enemy and now when the enemy is in a much greater force and nearer than he had been at any time, the whole of my mobile force, is withdrawn, not only from the vicinity of the mines, but right out of the district, Kakamas being 80 miles east of the north-east border of my district (lat 90 - 20, long 29 - 30). Regarding the defence of Namaqualand I have already explained the dangerous situation here and appeal to you to send more troops as quickly as possible. I cannot speak too highly of the work done by the Namaqualand Town Guard Battalion under the command of Major J.L. Dean. They constructed the excellent defences of O'Okiep and Port

Nolloth entirely, and have been periodically employed on permanent duty. At the same time they require a stiffening of regular NCO's which I am unable to provide now the troops have been withdrawn. The Namaqualand Border Scouts were raised with the object of forming a screen by means of a chain of cossack posts and patrols from the Orange River on the northern border down the eastern and southern areas to the mouth of Brak River on the sea coast. The withdrawal of this corps from the district leaves the entire border unprotected, and there is nothing to prevent the enemy now marching clean through the district, pillaging villages, cutting the railway (our one source of obtaining supplies) by burning the wooden viaducts at Klipfontein, and destroying the railway depot, and rolling stock of the company at Port Nolloth where there is now only a company of Town Guards, 2/3rds coloured men. At Garies there is a large quantity of grain collected by Colonel White and left there by him owing to want of transport to remove it. There are large quantities of dynamite in the district, used by the copper companies in their mining work and stored in magazines along the railway. I have no means of safeguarding this, short of destroying it or removing it to ships at Port Nolloth. The former would greatly inconvenience the copper companies in carrying on their work. This causes me some anxiety. The Mission stations of Steinkopf, Komaggas, Liliesfontein and Concordia are all unprotected and in the event of an invasion in force, would in all probability be roughly handled by the rebels, as each of these Missions has contributed largely in providing recruits for the NBS, a corps against which the enemy has evinced peculiar vindictiveness in flogging and shooting unfortunate prisoners who fell into their hands. The stock collected by Colonel White's column now grazing at Komaggas and Henkriesfontein is unprotected and quite at the mercy of the enemy. I have consulted Colonel White and in view of the situation as it now stands he considers I am justified in applying for reinforcements which I trust the GOC may be able to send me at an early date. Colonel White told me before he left he would support my application. If they can be spared I should by glad of two strong companies of Infantry with two Maxims and a gun boat sent to Port Nolloth. I regret to have to report very unfavourably on the state of wells and water holes in Bushmanland, and on the lines of communication with Colonel White's column, Lieutenant Thornton of the Northumberland Fusiliers, who has just come in from Bushmanland, reports water low in all wells, some dry and others full of dead animals. I anticipate very great difficulty in keeping Colonel White's column supplied at such a distance from base - 180 miles over a roadless and waterless desert, and fear the mortality amongst transport animals will be heavy (oxen and mules). I have pushed forward supplies - stores and forage - to last the column to middle of January, but find it very difficult to obtain wagons owing to the bad condition of the oxen, the result of the drought and absence of grazing. Mules are useless across the sand dunes, and there is no water there. Unfortunately there is a plentiful supply of water in the Sand Veldt - the tract of country between O'Okiep and Hondeklip Bay, the route the enemy will assuredly take, should they

*A group of Non-commissioned Officers at O'Okiep 3rd Bn.
The Queen's Royal West Surrey Regiment.*

make an incursion into the district from the south with the object of cutting the railway. Colonel White's column left yesterday for Nous and Kakamas. I have called out a portion of the Town Guard for permanent duty numbering about 4 to 6 officers and 80 to 100 men during the absence of the column." --- Signed W. Shelton.

This message was sent by the German steamer *Gertrude Woermann* on the 21st December, 1901 from Port Nolloth, due Cape Town 23rd.

It was now Christmas Day and peace and quiet prevailed at the mining centre, with all the inhabitants, including many Cornish miners, celebrating this Christian holiday. The situation at the end of December, 1901, was not a cheerful one for Shelton. The Boer commandos had succeeded in penetrating well into Namaqualand. General Smuts had managed to obtain a substantial number of volunteers throughout the Cape and was soon to advance towards Okiep and the mining towns.

Accordingly Shelton had enrolled a further 170 Border Scouts and organized these men into the 2nd Battalion NBS. However, he was still desperately short of NCO's to train them. Of the new men under his command he had left 70 at Garies with Lieutenant Hodge (NBS) in defence of that town, with a further 50 constructing blockhouses on the railway - all of whom were armed - and a further 50 were augmenting the Namaqualand Town Guard Battalion for the defence of the village and mine at Concordia. More intelligence reports confirmed he was now cut off from a Mission station at Leliefontein where the Boers were patrolling. Another report stated that Bowesdorp had been entered by a commando, strength about 50, and a store looted. The telegraph wire to Garies had again been cut and there was no post cart operating to the British garrison.

Shelton was now relying completely on sea communication. *HMS Barracouta* that arrived on the evening of 29th December at Port Nolloth, had left without either warning or giving the Commandant at the Port time to send letters and telegrams which were from Shelton and were awaiting a ship.

Billy Cook, one of Shelton's scouts, had managed to give Shelton some information on a strong patrol of Boers (about 50) that was within a reasonable distance to the south of Okiep. This was probably the same commando of 100 that had crossed the Garies-Hondeklip Bay road on the night of December 29th. This group appeared to be heading north in the neighbourhood of Leliefontein. Their leader was General S.G. Maritz who had also sent a patrol as far as Spetakel where there was a copper mine and probably some dynamite.

The little outpost at Garies reported all well and in good spirits when the last message got through, the telegraph wire having been severed at 2.55pm on the 30th December 1901. The small garrison was confident of holding out against a stronger force and was digging in. A little fort of boulders and rocks had been built in a strategic position, with a look-out post some distance away, and was ready for any action. Meanwhile, back on the railway line north of Okiep, Shelton had completed the building of two blockhouses which would defend the important wooden viaducts near Anenous. There were also two blockhouses at Nababeep, to the west of Okiep, which were to help defend the mine, water supplies, and smelting works. This area was manned by a company of NTGB. Additionally, Shelton had constructed two blockhouses at Concordia which were to be defended by the Town Guard.

At Springbokfontein there were three blockhouses manned by volunteers mostly government officials and store keepers. Using the 3rd Queens and local volunteers, Colonel Shelton had done everything he could to ensure the best possible defence of the mining area, but to protect and patrol the vast district for which he was responsible was a monumental task. General Smuts and his officers were aware of the defence arrangements. Smuts had already sent out scouts to observe the British outposts which he was soon to attack. The highly disciplined and experienced commando had ridden a long way and was now determined to see their cause triumph. This was a vital period of the war during which unique and historic events were to take place - many of which are now recorded here for the first time.

Intelligence received of Boer presence at Pella

CHAPTER 5

GARIES CUT OFF

Colonel White and his mobile column arrived in Nous on the morning or the 27th December where he immediately took two local 'rebels' prisoner. They had in their possession three rifles, seven horses and two saddles. After interrogating them White sent word that Jan Louw's commando, numbering 400 men, was at Brabees, 20 miles west of Kakamas. This position, he said, was too strong to be taken by frontal attack. Apart from that, there was no water for 30 miles. He considered the risk, and decided to move on to Kenhardt, where he expected to arrive on the evening of the 31st December. There he would fill his wagons, borrow what troops he could, and endeavour to obtain further support from the Officer Commanding the North-West District at Upington. He would then attack Louw from the east.

The two prisoners had said that many of Louw's men had tried to cross into German territory, but the Germans would not allow anyone to pass either way, except at Ramans Drift. There was also a strong German patrol at Schuit Drift, maintaining a close watch on the area.

Back in Okiep Shelton was now loading up a strong convoy of supplies to support Colonel White's column. This was also risky as there was nothing to prevent a strong Boer patrol intercepting it en route. He had no troops to escort the convoy as the nearest were at Pofadder 135 miles from his headquarters. However, he decided to send the convoy out, hoping it would arrive safely. On the 29th December, Shelton received a telegram from Major Parson of the 3rd Queens at De Aar which arrived via *HMS Barracouta* from Port Nolloth. It said; "Colonel Fairtlough has unfortunately been invalided back to England with acute rheumatism and that there are two Companies of Queens at Prieska. At HQ - 3 officers and 31 men (De Aar) the rest distributed on railway line. At HQ here am taking command - subject to your approval."

Although Shelton was second in command of the 3rd Battalion (Queens) he desperately wanted to stay at his headquarters at Okiep where he now had vast knowledge of the country under his command and had done much to protect the important copper mining centre, the railway and Port Nolloth. He accordingly sent a message to General Settle in Cape Town requesting authority to remain Commandant of Namaqualand, which Settle approved. Major Parson then assumed command of the detachment at De Aar.

Captain MacDonald, who arrived from Cape Town on January 2nd, 1902, was of great assistance to Shelton. This officer was an experienced soldier and a highly skilled horseman. He at once took out a patrol of local volunteers towards Komaggas where he unfortunately ran straight into a strong patrol of Boers who were holding a kopje. MacDonald opened fire immediately as his patrol spread out to take cover. The fight then developed into a bloody and bitter skirmish for some time until MacDonald gave the order to charge the position, which resulted in one of the enemy being killed and two

73

wounded. The remaining Boers broke off the conflict and disappeared into the veld. Unfortunately other volunteer troops who had been captured during the skirmish had been shot - 2 dead, 2 inhumanely flogged. (This was reported by MacDonald to Shelton on the 2nd January 1902.) When Capt MacDonald returned to Okiep headquarters he had managed to recruit a further fifty-five volunteers from the Kamaggas area.

The time had now come for Shelton to inspect the entire defence system on the important railway from Okiep to Port Nolloth (length ninety-one and a half miles.) On Tuesday January 14th he left his HQ to check the blockhouse constructions on this vital link with the port. Everything was going well. He had sufficient men to man the posts at vulnerable points. Especially important were the wooden viaducts at Anenous. The water station at Steinkopf was protected, and at Klipfontein a second blockhouse was completed which covered the railway line. Continuing down the Klipfontein Mountain Shelton inspected the two blockhouses which were situated at either end of the wooden viaduct.

Further along the railway, and not far from the Port were two blockhouses at Oojabies and Jules Hoogte, guarding the water supplies for Port Nolloth. At the Port itself Shelton had organized three strong blockhouses which were now complete. These covered the entrances to the Port in strategic positions (one having been sent direct from Cape Town in sections). A barbed wire fence was then erected round the Port completing the defence of Shelton's only sealink.

Suspected spy under arrest

Shelton then inspected the Town Guard who worked so hard on these fortifications and it was while he was there that *HMS Templehore* arrived bringing welcome supplies. The transport *Nautilus* was already there and she had also brought much needed rifles and ammunition. *Nautilus* brought Colonel Priestly, Major Logan RA, Major Edwards (an Australian) and Lieutenant Darter, who had brought with him a number of farriers, who were to work with the Namaqualand Border Scouts. Saddlery, the care of horses, ponies, mules and oxen were of paramount importance in this war. These animals were proving to be one of the greatest assets to both sides. Captain Ross (a member of Shelton's party) remained at Port Nolloth. Shelton, together with the new arrivals returned to his HQ at Okiep.

Shelton was delighted to have with him Colonel Priestly, who was an expert on defence works. Majors Edwards and Logan were both highly experienced in artillery and explosives. While the Boers, under the command of General Smuts, drew closer, Shelton reviewed his plan for the defence of the whole area. Certainly the defence of the railway was going to be a difficult task, as Smuts and his commando units were soon to prove.

Doctor Howard, Medical Officer, 3rd Queen's and
Shelton's unofficial photographer

One of the characteristics of Smut's commando was its swiftness in moving from area to area avoiding the main British army columns.

Meanwhile Lieutenant Hodges who was holding Garies, had managed to get a runner through to Shelton on the 20th January, who brought various reports, one of which said 150 Boers were situated north of the Green River and had trekked north from Biesiesfontein in two large patrols with wagons and carts. On the 18th a further 150 trekked from Grootbrakfontein towards Garies with the intention of attacking the outpost, but they sighted a British patrol led by Lieutenant Macintyre from Bowesdorp and quickly diverted to Skuinskraal. Reports also indicated 50 Boers were at Haas River - these men endeavoured to ambush Macintyre's patrol but were detected and retired when fired upon. It was becoming clear to Shelton that it was Smuts' intention to concentrate his force somewhere in the North-West Cape.

The fitness of the 3rd Queens, who were with Colonel White's column, was demonstrated by Private Smith, who escaped from the Boers after an engagement. He had walked in his socks from Brabees to Pofadder - a distance of 35 miles - and was now back at Okiep, giving vital intelligence to Shelton while the Medical Officer attended to his badly swollen and lacerated feet. At the same time, good news came in from White confirming that the convoy sent out by Shelton had arrived safely. Consequently, Colonel White had carried out some sorties to seek out Louw and attack him. White confirmed that his area was clear of the enemy and therefore he was returning to HQ leaving outposts at various points which would cover any Boer advance from the east on the Okiep garrison.

Shelton was delighted to hear that White was returning with the column, for this meant that his mobile troops would once again be back at HQ in Okiep and available for the defence of the mining town. He had previously asked General Settle at Cape Town for reinforcements of two more companies of Infantry but he considered this was not now necessary. He confirmed this by a message sent via the German steamer *Gertrude Woermann* which sailed from Port Nolloth at 6pm on the 19th January 1901 for Cape Town.

Colonel White who was now on his way back to Okiep, sent a runner ahead to report that on the 12th and 15th January he had been in action against General H.W. Lategan and his rebels between Kakamas and Kenhardt, and had sustained certain casualties. They were: Cpl White NBS (killed), and three other men. Captain Montague, Lieutenant Maddison and 12 men wounded. Boer casualties were unknown. White asked Shelton to stand by with medical staff and his doctor to meet the column as soon as sighted. However, the return trek was delayed by slow movement of the wagons carrying the wounded men, most of whom were suffering badly as the wagons were pulled slowly on the rough terrain. To add to their trials White's men were constantly sniped at by invisible Boers who could not be located when pursued. The Mauser rifles used by the Boers were able to pick off a target at amazing distances. On hearing the news Colonel Shelton sent out Captain Williamson (3rd Queens) supported by a handful of NBS to endeavour to locate White who may have had to alter his course back to Okiep now that Lategan and his men were in the vicinity.

On the 20th January, Shelton was informed that a patrol of Boers had entered the mission station at Leliefontein. Another Boer patrol had arrived at Koornhuis (four hours south of Springbok) with a smaller group entering Taaibosch Hoek. They were desperately short of proper clothing and food which was given to them by the local Afrikaans people in addition to much needed forage for their horses.

Shelton was becoming very concerned with the overall situation in his district. Accordingly he again decided to advise his General in Cape Town asking for the communication to be urgently sent on to General French at Middelburg. On January 26th, 1902 he sent the following message:

"The enemy has now penetrated my district south, isolating Garies and cutting the telegraph line. Some 300 are reported between that place and Bowersdorp. Small patrols are reported both to the east of Post Cart Road in neighbourhood of Kakamas and Spectakel on the west. Farms belonging to the Roux's at Silverfontein and Rietfontein 12 and 18 miles east of Springbok, were visited last night, and the Boers carried off John Roux and a scout. Yesterday midday, this patrol (about 20) was reported a few miles east of O'OKiep but my patrols I sent out failed to locate them. On my N.E. border the enemy is reported in force in the neighbourhood of Kakamas. At present in absence of my mobile troops with Colonel White's column I am occupying O'OKiep with the Town Guard, a small detachment of CGA and half a company of 5th Royal Warwicks which arrived yesterday. I have now a small number of these men occupying the blockhouses at Springbok and Town Guards at Concordia and Nababeep with small posts furnished by mounted men of NBS from Concordia to Nababeep in a chain circling round Springbok. I also have a small post at Ramans Drift. Colonel White dropped an officer and 50 men at Pofadder outside my N.E. Border. There is also a strong detachment of Town Guard garrisoning Port Nolloth.

"The Blockhouses along the railway line - O'OKiep to Port Nolloth - (91½ miles) are fully manned. The enemy could advance through the Sand Veld with the object of cutting the railway and telegraph wire and destroying the viaducts towards Klipfontein. The holding of the waterholes in Bushmanland is of paramount importance. I am of the opinion that further blockhouses should be constructed at Vallekrall east of Hondeklip Bay (to be supplied from latter port), Specktakel and Kamaggas - more should be built at Rozynbosch, Aggenhuis and Naroep, and all important waterholes, and then held by us which would prevent any attack from north-east as there is no water between Aggenhuis and Kaitob a distance of 60 miles. This would protect the railway on the east and the south.

*A company of the 3rd Queen's, **en route** to Okiep,
filling their water bottles*

"I am quite alive to the importance of this post, practically the key to Bushmanland, but it is out of my district and a very long way for me to supply Namies as an alternative post. I should not be surprised if Colonel White dropped posts at some of these places. I am writing him by special despatch and hope to intercept him on his return journey." Signed W. Shelton Situation at 26.1.1902. Sent by *Nautilus* 27.1.02

Martial Law which Shelton had established throughout the entire district of Namaqualand of 20th January 1901, was being strictly enforced. He was successful in this respect owing to the large British community and the extreme loyalty of the 'Bastard' element.

He was receiving good co-operation from all Civil Officers and the officials of the important Cape Copper Company and Namaqua Copper Company and in addition to them there were the missionaries and the majority of the local farmers. Bearing in mind that the population of the area was 17,000, he considered the fact that only 83 men who had joined the rebels confirmed the loyalty of the people of Namaqualand. However, there was a strong tendency to sympathize with the Boers on the part of the purely Dutch who were being coerced by the advancing commandos. One of the difficulties

Funeral of a trooper killed serving with Colonel White's column

79

Shelton had was with the majority of the field-cornets (junior officers appointed by commandants who had the power to commandeer anything in their district). Many of them had failed to carry out his orders and in various instances had misled him especially over the location of horses in their immediate area. The result being that these much needed animals had fallen into the hands of the Boers. These field-cornets had many plausible excuses and it was difficult for Shelton to bring charges against them owing to the reluctance of the farmers and natives to swear affidavits against them. With the absence of troops in the district he was bound to rely on the field-cornets to assist him in collecting horses and other animals. He was of the opinion that the majority of these men were ill-chosen and unsuited for the post. Their one object in mind was their fees. Very few spoke English and most were untrustworthy. Shelton believed a radical change was needed in this department as he said; "None should be appointed that cannot speak the language of his adopted country."

The Bubonic plague which had broken out in Cape Town in March 1901 had, through the efforts of Colonel Shelton and his MO, been kept out of Namaqualand, although strict quarantine regulations were still in force. Unfortunately the plague was taking its toll in the Southern Cape area and especially in the British Concentration Camps where the majority of deaths involved women and children. There was no local newspaper or printed news of any kind in Okiep or Namaqualand, so Shelton had to type all notices

Pay day for the Namaqualand Border Scouts and the Okiep Town Guard

and proclamations for distribution in the area. News from the outside world came only via Port Nolloth when either the *Nautilus* or *Gertrude Woermann* arrived monthly from Cape Town.

The Boer advance towards Okiep and the copper mining area was now considered extremely serious. Intelligence sent Shelton a full report indicating that General Smuts' commandos had joined up and were sending out strong patrols to watch the mobile columns from the Okiep HQ. General Smuts had concentrated his men in the Kamiesberg and Bowesdorp areas. With him now were Maritz, C. Schoeman, Van Deventer, Bouwer and J.L. Theron. The estimated numbers of experienced commandos was now about 3,000 all of whom were prepared to fight to the last man for their cause. They had come a long way and although many wore mere sacking for clothing, and make shift dress, and managed to secure food, ammunition and some new horses, they were desperate men hoping they would eventually win the war.

Okiep Town Guard on the march
By courtesy of O'OKiep Copper Company

Colonel White, who had arrived safely back in Okiep had been ordered out again after resting. This time he took a stronger mobile force towards Mesklip to a supply depot. His strength consisted of 15 officers and 364 other ranks, including 346 horses and one nine pounder Field gun. White now had a detachment of the 5th Battalion, the Royal Warwickshire Regiment with him, who had considerable fire power. As Colonel White's column approached Mesklip (23 miles to the south of Spektakel), a scout rode up to report that a dead body had been found a short distance ahead. It was that of Trooper Stephen Ramsden (unarmed), the bearer of a despatch from the Department Commandant of Spektakel. He had been shot through the head. His horse had been recognised with a party of Boers who had raided Komaggas some days earlier. White ordered the body to be taken back to Okiep HQ where Colonel Shelton arranged for a post mortem to be carried out by Dr Howard. Some hours later the advance scouts of White's column sighted a large body of the enemy but they withdrew towards the Buffel River when the saw the main strength of the British column. On hearing the news of the concentration of Boers, Shelton hastily sent out a back-up convoy some hours after White left Okiep. This consisted of some 174 mules, 352 oxen with 44 wagons of supplies. It was his intention to keep up a continuous run to Mesklip where White would then press on to Garies after building up the depot. However, the condition of many of the animals was giving cause for concern owing to the lack of grazing. There was none in the immediate neighbourhood. So it was decided to send the oxen to

Young members of the 3rd Queen's having a morning wash at Okiep

Kweekfontein to graze. These were sent without any strong escort but with White's men covering the area, Shelton considered there was little risk of attack.

On February 24th, 1902, Shelton temporarily evacuated 10 of the 13 blockhouses which covered the approaches to the Mining Centre (Okiep) north and south. Colonel White was forming a screen between Okiep and Smuts' commando who were now moving in rapidly. White pushed forward the detachment of the 5th Warwicks to Mesklip and further on towards the towns of Bowesdorp and Garies.

In Garies, Lieutenant Hodges was holding the town against numerous Boer patrols which he and his men shot at when they ventured too close. Although the Boer commandos were very much in force throughout the area, Hodges got a message through the enemy lines by duplicate runners. Both arrived safely. The messages, which gave vital information of Boer commando movements to Shelton, were written on tissue paper and then typed out in the Headquarters.

In the Okiep area, a train got through to Shelton's HQ from Port Nolloth with letters, parcels, newspapers and other supplies. By Wednesday, March 26th, the situation was becoming worse each day for the British Mining area. Shelton sent another urgent letter to his CO in Cape Town - Major General Sir Henry Settle KCP, DSO:

"The whole southern portion of this district is swarming with Boers - the country has been cleared of stock and grain and horses but there has been a severe drought consequently much suffering to the inhabitants and the animals has resulted. The whole of my mobile force is lost to me for defence purposes for which it was organized. The men of the Namaqualand Town Guard Battalion are virtually breaking down under the strain of the excessive work they have lately done owing to the removal of the legitimate garrison. I cannot relax their duties in the last degree as the enemy would certainly attack the place. It is inexplicable to me why they have not done so already. At Concordia and Nababeep they don't like the blockhouses and funk the mines I fancy, as these cover the approaches. My greatest fear is the railway line being cut in which case our only other source of supply would be severed. I am now organizing a Pigeon Post to Port Nolloth in case we become isolated. I am extremely loth to close the mines here in O'OKiep, Concordia and Nababeep, which would greatly inconvenience the Cape Copper Company, who have given me every assistance since the day I arrived. If I did order the mines to stop work it would throw some 3,000 people out of employment, and I would have to feed them. The Copper Companies only pay their employees for work actually carried out. The work force have no other means of subsistence. At the present time I consider I have sufficient supplies to keep 1,000 people including my troops for about three months, but any moment now this number might well be trebled or more by refugees coming in owing to the advance of the Boer commando. Summing up - I would frankly say this - Colonel White with main portion of the Namaqualand Field Force, numbering 550 officers and men, with a similar number of horses, is now in Garies, with a fortnight or three weeks supplies. About 1,500 of the enemy under Generals Smuts, Maritz and Schoeman are between Garies and O'OKiep.

"O'OKiep, Concordia and Nababeep are certainly fortified and garrisoned by the Town Guards, but the men are worn out by pressure of work and duties. The railway is inadequately guarded by some untrained scouts whose engagement may terminate tomorrow many of whom are leaving to plough, and are at the mercy of the enemy in the absence of my main regular force of troops.

"As I calculate the value of the property committed to my charge by the Mining Companies i.e. (1) The Cape Copper Company, (2) Namaqua Copper Company, SA Copper Company and Namaqua Ventuer Syndicate, added to the railway and rolling stock, Depot work Port Nolloth of the Cape Copper Company to be worth at a low estimate of £1 million and a half sterling. I feel reinforcements should be sent immediately." Signed Shelton.

Officers' kitchen and chef in the veld

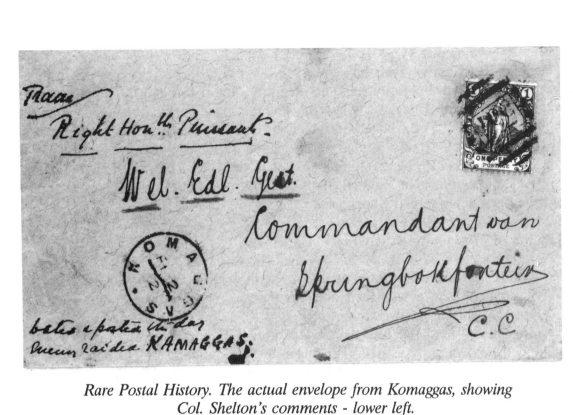

Rare Postal History. The actual envelope from Komaggas, showing
Col. Shelton's comments - lower left.

3rd Queen's firing on Boer patrol near Okiep

The fact that Boer activity was now spread over a very large area was confirmed to Shelton when, on 26th February 1902, he received a letter through the post cart system from the small town of Komaggas (where in 1860 the first Civil Commissioner appointed had his seat). This letter contained a Proclamation written in High Dutch and signed by Chief Commandant C.R. de Wet and notice signed by Field-General S.G. Maritz. On translation it appeared to be the Boer's answer to the British Martial Law regulations. It is interesting to note that Colonel Shelton has written on the envelope "Dated and posted the day enemy raided Kamaggas."

Translation of Proclamation signed by C.R. de Wet.

"Whereas it had been brought to my attention that the British Military Commanders have published and circulated certain notices among the Boer population to force them to do war service. Whereas the Federal forces had already been in the Cape Colony for more than eight months and have occupied districts and the military Command of His Majesty, notwithstanding that they could have given the necessary protection to the peaceful inhabitants of the country, they nevertheless have taken from the farms, the horses, fodder and grain to be taken to military stations or towns.

They also expected from the inhabitants that they should report and spy upon the movements of the Federal Forces
"And whereas it could not be allowed that people be peaceful one day, and the next day engage in acts of war. So it is that I, Christian Rudolph de Wet, Chief Commandant of the Orange Free State Armed Forces, declare as follows:

"A.   That any person, who is not of Her Majesty's Forces and is found guilty of providing food or horses to any military station or town, will be sentenced to a penalty of £50 (maximum). By non-payment the Commanding Officer will have the power to confiscate moving property from the guilty party to the value of the penalty.

"B.   Any person not with Her Majesty's Forces, who gives direct, or indirect information about the movement, numbers or any other information about the Federal Forces to the British Military Forces, will be sentenced to a maximum penalty of £2,000 sterling. On non-payment, the Commanding Officer could confiscate moving property of the guilty party to the value of the penalty.

"C.   Any person who is found guilty of espionage against the Federal Forces, will immediately be brought before a Council of War Court Martial (consisting of one Chief Officer and two others). If he is found guilty, he will be strictly dealt with. Any other proclamation by any other officer in respect of the above is hereby repealed.

"Signed under my hand at Senekal, Orange Free State on the 24th day of August 1901.

C.R. de Wet
Chief Commandant of the OFS Armed Forces.

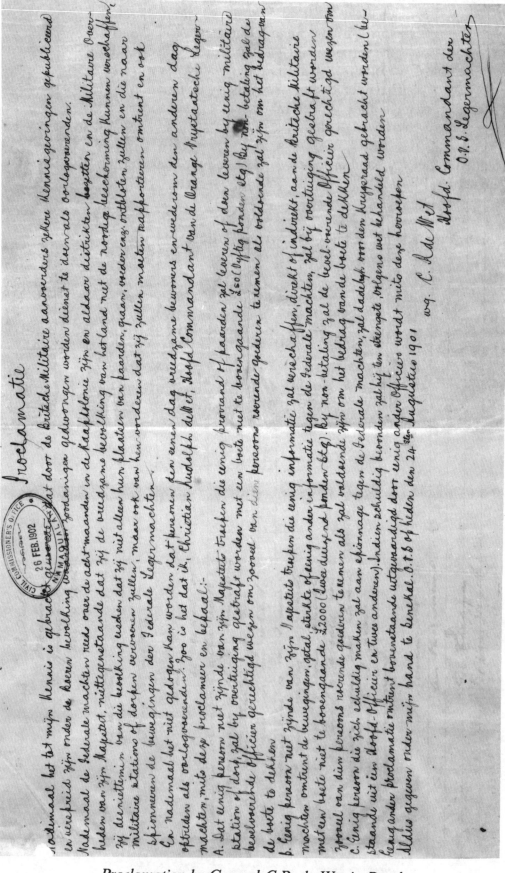

Proclamation by General C.R. de Wet in Dutch

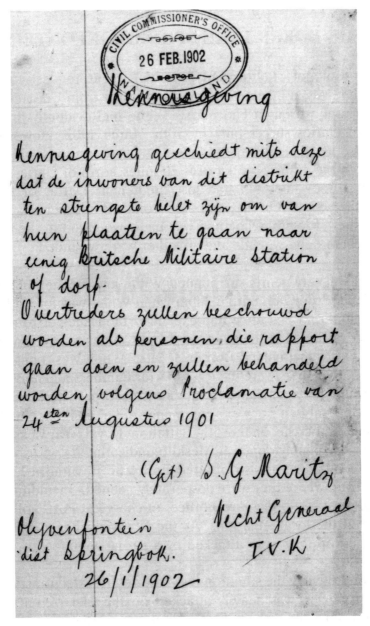

Additional notice adjioning the proclamation signed by S.G. Maritz.

English translation: NOTICE: Notice is hereby given that the inhabitants of the district are strictly forbidden to leave their farms and go to any British military station or town. Trespassers would be regarded as messengers and they would be dealt with according to the Proclamation of 24 August 1901.

Signed: S.G. Maritz
      Combat General
      TVK
Olyvenfontein
dist: Springbok
26.1.1902

CHAPTER 6

THE BOERS TAKE SPRINGBOKFONTEIN

A few days after Colonel Shelton had sent his urgent request to Cape Town for reinforcements, he received by native runner a message from Colonel White. It was of extreme seriousness and brought bad news. White had evidently managed to get the convoy through to Garies successfully by 10th March 1902. However, he had been strongly opposed by the Boers in large numbers on his return to Rietkloof where a fierce battle took place on the 16th. (Rietkloof is 20 miles north of Garies.) White forced a wedge through the Boer lines but had lost Lieutenant Darter of the Namaqualand Border Scouts in the action. On the Boer side Comdt Boonzaier was severely wounded and died shortly after. Comdt Schoeman was badly wounded in the buttocks and F.C. van Zitters had severe head wounds and six other were wounded.

On the 19th the Boers very nearly surrounded White and his men in a basin north of a pass. The fight lasted from 7am until 6.30pm when White was forced back to Garies to replenish his ammunition. His force had expended thousands of rounds at the enemy. Sergeant Bidmead was killed in the action and Cpl Kenney received wounds to the leg - both members of the Namaqualand Border Scouts. White was trying to rejoin Shelton by the Sandveld but the Boers were in very superior numbers and about 400 had arrived with wagons of wounded which came from Vanrhynsdorp. These were reported to be men serving with General Ben Bouwer's commando. Shelton immediately sent an urgent warning to Captain Lutwyche of the 5th Battalion Royal Warwicks, who had half a Company guarding the supply depot at Mesklip, indicating he was soon to be attacked by Smuts' commando. Shelton also ordered Lutwyche to withdraw with his men and supplies back to Okiep where they were desperately needed. In addition to this, Shelton despatched a vital message to the Naval officer in charge at Port Nolloth giving him an up to date report of the local situation. As the Warwicks began to pull out from the supply depot at Mesklip they were attacked by a strong commando under Maritz.

From Shelton's point of view the situation had now deteriorated drastically. White, now virtually cut off in Garies, was heavily attacked on the 21st March by stronger Boer forces, but they retired after a short engagement to maintain a constant watch on the British column. This commando unit was led by Maritz. Smuts was now near Bethel, fourteen miles north of Garies, holding the district road and covering the western road. He had about 1,000 men with him who had re-grouped in the Kamiesberg which had been previously reported clear by Colonel White. Shelton realized now that his main force of defence troops were shut up in Garies, and his only regular force would be half a company of 5th Battalion Royal Warwicks who were now fighting their way back to Okiep. These troops, supported by the Town Guard and men of the Cape Garrison Artillery, plus the local mine volunteers, were going to be Shelton's only defence of the important mining headquarters.

He had thirteen blockhouses to man and was going to be forced to use the coloured men of the Town Guard to help the Royal Warwicks to defend them. It was a turn about situation for Shelton. He had already considered evacuating Springbokfontein,

90

Cape Town District Office,

Main Barracks, Cape Town,

......21st.March.., 190 2.

Dear Colonel Shelton,

Many thanks for your letter of the
15th instant. I am very glad to hear you give such a good
account of Namaqualand, and that the Loyalists in that
Country are fully able to hold their own.
Now that we have established Martial Law for some months
in Cape Town, I believe that the coast trade will be under
better control, and if you put your Commandant at Port
Nolloth in communication with the Assistant Commandant of
the Docks, (Lieut.Lingham, R.N.,) I think we shall have no
future difficulty as far as Namaqualand is concerned.
You must have enjoyed your 12 hours on board the "Canada"
in meeting old friends.

As a whole things are going very well, and though the
war is not yet at an end, I do not think the end is very
far distant. A good deal is made by the Boers and their
friends of slight reverses which are unavoidable when
small Columns are working over wide Districts. They may
for the moment cause a little delay, but do not effect the
ultimate result.

If at any time I can do anything for you, please
let me know.

Believe me,

Yours Sincerely,

*Personal letter from Colonel Cooper in Cape Town to Colonel Shelton
March 21st 1902. At the time Cooper wrote this he was unaware of the
dangerous situation in Namaqualand.*

Concordia and Nababeep, which would at least give him the support of those Town Guards, and the firepower of many more rifles, which was essential, but it would also entail feeding up to 6,000 people.

His next message to General French in Cape Town requested more reinforcements, with as many horses as possible. It was going to be difficult to land horses at Port Nolloth and the use of 'slings' would be the only method from smaller vessels which could enter the port more easily owing to the shallow approach. Neither the *Nautilus* nor the German vessel, *Gertrude Woermann*, were in at Port Nolloth at this time. The text of Shelton's message was:

"To: General Settle and French (Copy to Intelligence) Cape Town, forwarded to Lamberts Bay by CCC Tug *Gnu* to be transmitted by SNO by **quickest route to C.T. Tug left Port Nolloth at midnight on 26th March 1902**. Since receiving White's despatch my Intelligence Scouts have brought in information corroborating White's report regarding strength of enemy in Kamiesberg and neighbourhood of Bowersdorp. As I have no mobile forces to attempt in any way to relieve White at Garies and do not consider I am strong enough to hold O'OKiep now the entire Namaqualand Field Force is lost to me, I hope the re-enforcements I previously asked for may be sent quickly or the valuable mining property together with the 'rolling stock', and the large quantity of military stores and ammunition with three guns, may fall into the hands of the enemy. The strength of present Garrison here is CGA 1 officer and 26 men with a 9 pounder ML Field Gun and 2 Maxims. Town Guard 13 officers and 312 of which 97 are white men of which again 24 are non-effective owing to sickness and duty on the railway, and the depot of NBS. The Town Guard are fairly worn out with incessant blockhouse and picquet duties. Many of the whites are old men over 60 years of age and cannot stand the work any longer tho' they have stuck it pluckily so far. I have 13 blockhouses to man and have difficulties with the coloured men of the Town Guard who need some more training.

"As there is little likelihood of Colonel White getting out of Garies for some time I am withdrawing the post at Mesklip which is threatened by General Smuts with a very strong force of experienced commandos. I am bringing in the stores left there by Colonel White. If enemy advances much further I shall be compelled to evacuate Springbokfontein and Concordia both vulnerable mining areas and concentrate in O'OKiep. This will entail feeding a large community so I hope you will be able to send me considerable supplies as soon as possible say for 3,000 to 4,000 people for three months. I have no horses to mount troops when you reinforce me. Tho' difficult, it will be possible to land horses at Port Nolloth providing you send slings and expert men to land them. As there is no ship in and *Nautilus* may not be in for about a week I have commandeered the Cape Copper Company's tug *Gnu* and am sending this to Lamberts Bay to Senior Naval Officer to forward to Cape Town by fast

Men of the 5th Battn. Royal Warwickshire Regt. falling back on O'OKiep under attack.

Boer Leader Stenekamp involved in first action at Grootkau.

Torpedo Boat. I trust you will consider the great importance of the news and the seriousness of the situation justifies the course I have adopted. Please be good enough to confirm this! My estimate of Colonel White's column is about 500 men of all ranks and about 400 horses. I imagine he could hold out for about a fortnight - tho' he says nothing about this in his report.

"It would be impossible to supply him from here unless a column with guns was sent to me to get a convoy through. The railway once more is at the enemy's mercy although I have two blockhouses along the line guarding the important viaducts. My fear is these would not be strong enough against an attack in force. The enemy have wire entanglements just south of Bowersdorp."

Signed W, Shelton, 26 th March 1902

This was the beginning of events which led to a complete investment of the mining area by General Smuts.

General J.C. Smuts and Tottie Krige
By courtesy of W. Hancock Esq

94

The Cape Copper Company's tug *Gnu* was capable of a speed of seven knots under favourable circumstances, but the 'Bar' was up so she was forced to wait until midnight for a high tide before crossing and should normally have reached Lamberts Bay by noon on the 28th March, but Shelton had not received any word or news of her progress. He normally would receive information by district post, the sea and his intelligence agents which he had throughout the area. There was no telegraph link as this had been cut by his enemy. His agent at Ramans Drift had managed to send some news which had safely arrived from German South-West Africa. Another form of communication was by the steamer *Nautilus* from Cape Town, but this took much longer although at this particular stage of the campaign nothing was reliable.

Meanwhile the garrison at Garies had dug in. Colonel White's men consisted of the following; 11 officers, 55 Cape Garrison Artillery and Royal Warwicks, 116 NBS with 279 horses and 194 mules, one nine-pounder ML field gun, 17 wagons and one cart. The original small garrison which Shelton had left there under Lieutenant Hodges (NBS) with 2 officers of the Cape Garrison Artillery, plus 10 men of the 3rd Queen's supported by 155 Namaqualand Border Scouts and Town Guard 22, totalled 189 men with 48 horses. Unfortunately Shelton had no idea how much forage and stores Lieutenant Hodges had when White was forced back there, but he estimated with the totals - horses and men, including the townsfolk - White could hold out for about two weeks or three at the very most.

General Smuts was reconnoitring Bowersdorp with Schoeman and Bouwer, while Maritz kept White and his men busy at Garies. The stores at Mesklip had been safely brought back to Okiep and would contribute to the garrison's reserves. However, Shelton had left one blockhouse at Mesklip for intelligence purposes to which he had a connection by wire. The intelligence agents and scouts were covering the country to the south-east and west. The post was provisional for one month and had been supplied with plenty of water. It was situated in an impregnable location, being 25 miles south of Okiep, which meant Shelton was now in a position to receive early information that was going to prove invaluable to him.

With the Boer's advancing closer to his headquarters every day Shelton had requested an important cypher letter from the Resident Magistrate at Springbokfon-fontein. This code had been devised by the Military Intelligence Department and was used by Shelton for sending messages. The key to the cypher was taken from a page of the Victorian novel 'The Woman in White'. His telegraphist who was to send these important communica- tions was Miss Rowan who was now in Okiep Post Office awaiting his instructions.

The situation now extremely serious for Shelton prompted him to send out patrols from Okiep, Concordia, Nababeep and Springbokfontein to reconnoitre the areas where the movement of large numbers of Boers had been reported. He was hoping that the Cape Copper Company's tug *Gnu* had managed to get his message through to Cape Town, and that reinforcements would be on their way. On 21 March 1902 one of his patrols from Okiep reported that fierce fighting was taking place near Oogfontein, one hour's ride west of Garies and a further report stated that General Smuts with fifty men was at Koornhuis.

Cypher Letter

THE WOMAN IN WHITE. 167

This, in two words: He looks like a man who could tame anything. If he had married a tigress, instead of a woman, he would have tamed the tigress. If he had married me, I should have made his cigarettes as his wife does—I should have held my tongue when he looked at me, as she holds hers.

I am almost afraid to confess it, even to these secret pages. The man has interested me, has attracted me, has forced me to like him. In two short days, he has made his way straight into my favourable estimation—and how he has worked the miracle, is more than I can tell.

It absolutely startles me, now he is in my mind, to find how plainly I see him!—how much more plainly than I see Sir Percival, or Mr. Fairlie, or Walter Hartright, or any other absent person of whom I think, with the one exception of Laura herself! I can hear his voice, as if he was speaking at this moment. I knew what his conversation was yesterday, as well as if I was hearing it now. How am I to describe him? There are peculiarities in his personal appearance, his habits, and his amusements, which I should blame in the boldest terms, or ridicule in the most merciless manner, if I had seen them in another man. What is it that makes me unable to blame them, or to ridicule them in him?

For example, he is immensely fat. Before this time, I have always especially disliked corpulent humanity. I have always maintained that the popular notion of connecting excessive grossness of size and excessive good-humour as inseparable allies, was equivalent to declaring, either that no people but amiable people ever get fat, or that the accidental addition of so many pounds of flesh has a directly favourable influence over the disposition of the person on whose body they accumulate. I have invariably combated both these absurd assertions by quoting examples of fat people who were as mean, vicious, and cruel, as the leanest and the worst of their neighbours. I have asked whether Henry the Eighth was an amiable character? whether Pope Alexander the Sixth was a good man? Whether Mr. Murderer and Mrs. Murderess Manning were not both unusually stout people? Whether hired nurses, proverbially as cruel a set of women as are to be found in all England, were not, for the most part, also as fat a set of women as are to be found in all England?—and so on, through dozens of other examples, modern and ancient, native and foreign, high and low. Holding these strong opinions on the subject with might and main as I do at this moment, here, nevertheless, is Count Fosco, as fat as Henry the Eighth himself, established in my favour, at one day's notice, without let or hindrance from his own odious corpulence. Marvellous indeed!

Is it his face that has recommended him?

It may be his face. He is a most remarkable likeness, on a large scale, of the Great Napoleon. His features have Napoleon's magnificent regu

*Key to Shelton's cypher from
a page of* **The Woman in White**

Commandant Louis Wessels (seated) with his Secretary - R. MacDonald.

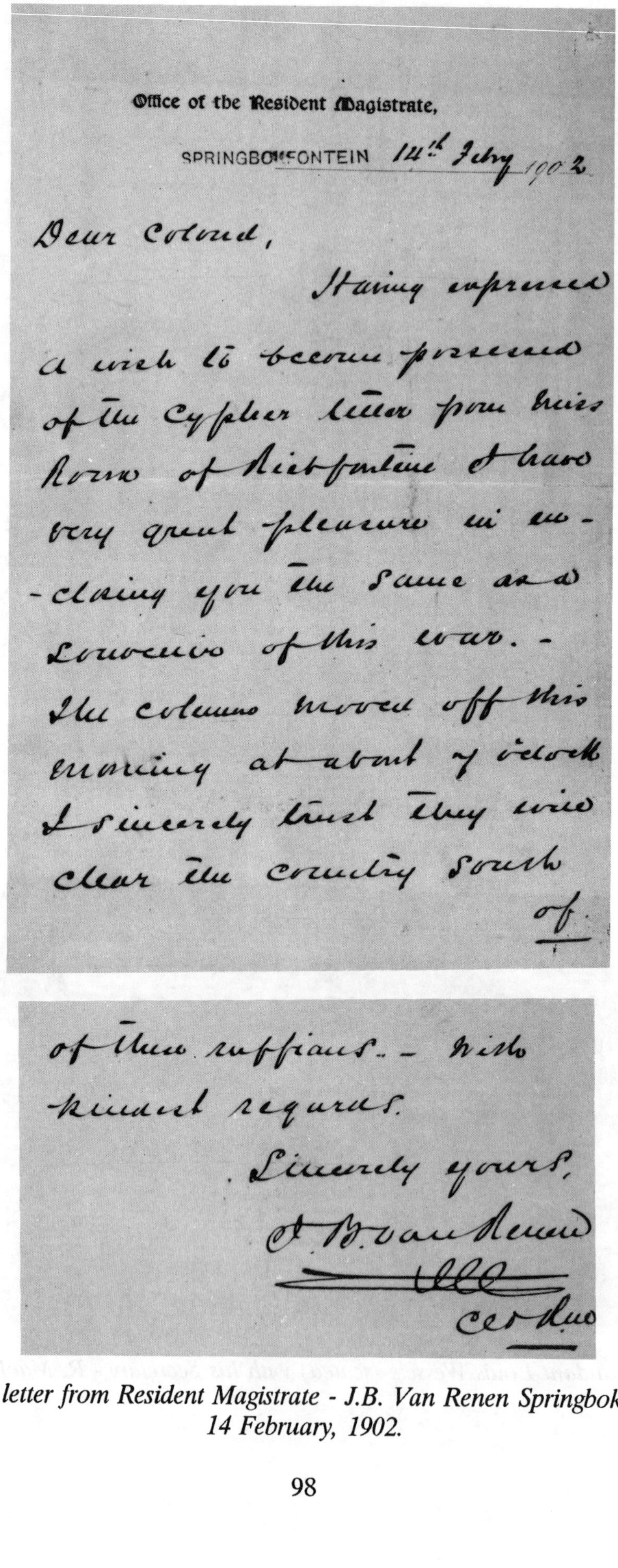

Office of the Resident Magistrate,

SPRINGBOKFONTEIN 14th Febry 1902.

Dear Colonel,

Having expressed a wish to become possessed of the Cypher letter from Miss Rouw of Nietfontein I have very great pleasure in enclosing you the same as a Souvenir of this war. –

The columns moved off this morning at about 7 o'clock. I sincerely trust they will clear the country south of

these ruffians. – With kindest regards.

Sincerely yours,

J. B. van Renen

cer Mag

Cypher letter from Resident Magistrate - J.B. Van Renen Springbokfontein
14 February, 1902.

98

On the 30th March, intelligence reports confirmed that General Smuts had left Bowersdorp on Tuesday, 25th March, moving north, and another force (identity unknown) had also moved in that direction on the same day. Two miles of telegraph line north of Bowersdorp had been destroyed by the Boers, which meant that this town and area was now completely cut off from communication with Okiep. On Sunday, 30th March, the detachment from Mesklip, which included one officer and 37 men of the 5th Battalion Royal Warwicks, finally arrived in Okiep. They had fought their way back to the headquarters, being attacked constantly from all sides by the Boer marksmen. Luckily, they had not suffered any fatal casualties but had brought with them several wounded men. With their withdrawal to Okiep, Shelton's garrison was now reinforced by British troops again and they were soon to prove their great value. On the same day, 30th March, at 8.30am, the *SS Nautilus* arrived from Cape Town and anchored off Port Nolloth. She brought more rifles and ammunition which were immediately loaded on the first train for Okiep. This consignment arrived in the mining headquarters at 6.30pm that same evening. The best news came when the Cape Copper Company's tug sailed into the Port at 11.30am confirming she had delivered Shelton's important message. Shelton recorded in his diary that the garrison of Okiep attended Divine Service and Holy Mass while the final preparations were being made for the defence of the town.

One of Shelton's local scouts

99

However, more grave news came in of an engagement of Lieutenant MacIntyre's patrol near Grootkou - 25 miles east of Okiep - at sunrise on the 31st March. First reports indicated Steenkamp's commando was involved, but it was not until 11.00am that an intelligence scout, Billy Cook, reported that the fight was still going on and there were dead and wounded on both sides. Thereafter, events developed rapidly, and it was reported that MacIntyre's patrol had been ambushed at Ratelkraal (north-east of Okiep). He and 3 wounded men were taken prisoner, ten of his men were killed and five seriously wounded had been left on the field. Two of the wounded had managed to get back to Concordia, bringing the bad news. The Boers numbered between 50 to 60 and were part of Steenkamp's commando from the Kenhardt district. This pointed to a concerted attack by the Boers from the direction of the north-eastern area.

At 6.40pm telegraphic communication with Mesklip was cut. Consequently, Shelton immediately sent out four native runners with enciphered orders to warn Springbokfontein, Concordia and Nababeep to be on the alert and expect imminent attack. The assault on the important mining area was about to begin.

It was Springbokfontein's turn first as General Smuts and his men moved in to surround the magisterial seat of Namaqualand which was protected by three blockhouses. These were manned by local volunteers - one of whom was the Resident Magistrate's clerk, Mr. Stewart. The first blockhouse was constructed on a very large mound just near a mine, and a barbed wire entanglement surrounding the building which was strategically placed to cover all directions of approach. Mr. Stewart was in command, ably supported by a young Dutch volunteer named Van Coevoerden, and another local man. The second blockhouse was situated a little distance away also on some raised ground. This too had a clear view of the town and was a formidable defensive position. Number three Fort was placed on a large rock which commanded the entire view of the town thereby giving a complete panoramic area of fire power. The Boers under the command of General Smuts attacked Springbokfontein with 300 men. Included in this force were two Irishmen by the names of Gallagher and Lang who had managed to locate some dynamite in a disused mine. Both these men were attached to General Ben Bouwer's commando and possessed a knowledge of explosives which they applied in making 'Dynamite hand grenades'. These new projectiles were going to be of great value to the Boers in the forthcoming conflict. As the Boers advanced towards the blockhouses, the two Irishmen, supported by a famous Boer commando named Deneys Reitz, selected blockhouse no. 1 as their primary target, but the first attempt to use the grenades was ineffective because they landed short of their target. The tremendous explosion which followed alerted the defenders who immediately opened fire. While Lang, Gallagher and Reitz, with others, were attacking blockhouse no. 1, the remaining Boers were also attacking forts no.2 and 3 with the dynamite bombs. A large explosion forced the occupants of blockhouse no. 2 to surrender. The bomb had been thrown by one Albert van Rooyen. Encouraged by this success the attackers decided to press home with more of the projectiles against fort no.3 which appeared to be the most difficult to reach. However, the Boers had managed to place bombs under part of the foundation of this blockhouse where they exploded with a great force, and a few minutes later blockhouse no.3 also surrendered. This then left blockhouse no.1 still holding out against superior odds. Nevertheless, just before the little garrison's heroic and stubborn resistance came

Commandant Louis Botha Commandant in Chief Boer Forces,
taken in the Eastern Transvaal with two Colleagues

to an end, they had managed to send up a rocket to warn Okiep of the attack. The time
was 4.10am when blockhouse no.1 surrendered. Mr. Stewart and H. Van Coevoerden
and a black man called Tehart lay dead inside the fortification. All three had been shot
through the head by Deneys Reitz who had been firing from a concealed position during
the attack. The brave defence of Springbokfontein was the first action in this war,
against an enemy using dynamite in the form of a grenade.

While the prisoners were being rounded up and taken to houses in the town for
questioning, General Smuts, with Van Deventer and Commandant Bouwer, had already
made plans to attack Concordia.

CHAPTER 7

THE SURRENDER OF CONCORDIA

The mining town of Concordia, situated some eight miles north-east of Okiep, was on the branch line of the Cape Copper Company's railway from Braakputs Junction near the main mining terminal. Captain F. Phillips was Deputy Commandant at Concordia and Superintendent of the Namaqua Copper Company which owned and worked the valuable mine at this location. The defence detachment there consisted of three officers and 125 other ranks who had been trained by the British troops which Colonel Shelton had sent to instruct the Town Guard in the use of arms and drill procedures. There was also a small detachment of Namaqualand Border Scouts who were similarly trained. Captain Wrentmore NTG Battalion was the Senior Officer but Phillips was a Justice of Peace and was also press censor, apart from his position as Deputy Commandant under the direct command of Colonel Shelton.

After the telegraph wire from Springbokfontein had been cut by the Boers at 4.05am on the morning of the 1st April, and no news having reached Okiep, Shelton decided to evacuate his two outer towns at Nababeep and Concordia. The people of Nababeep, receiving this order, began at once to leave their homes and travel into Okiep by train. The number soon increased as news spread quickly of the capture of Springbokfontein and the rapid advance of the Boer commandos. Shelton's problems, however, were just beginning. Captain Phillips at Concordia, on receiving the order to withdraw to Okiep, sent a signal to Shelton saying the garrison and the people would not leave their homes, although he had fully explained the situation they would be facing. The facts leading up to the surrender of Concordia to General Smuts' men are contained in signals from Shelton to Phillips:

> "**April 1st 8am** To Deputy Commandant Concordia from OC Namaqualand, O'OKiep. Enemy attacked Springbokfontein at 4am and wire cut immediately afterwards. I think the time has arrived for me in accordance with orders received from HQ to evacuate isolated towns and concentrate forces here. With this in view I am withdrawing the Nababeep Company of the Town Guards and bringing in as many of the inhabitants as may desire to come. It may be necessary to do the same with Concordia as I cannot run the risk of losing Government arms and ammunition. I think it would be advisable for Captain Phillips to ride in and confer with me this morning as to the steps to be taken. Meanwhile you will evacuate your distant blockhouse, bring in ammunition and stores and concentrate your force pending further orders from me in your village defence work. All saddlery, clothing, boots, horseshoes and anything likely to be of use to the enemy should be sent into O'OKiep. Preparation should be made to remove your women and children in case it becomes necessary. Natives might remain with safety at any rate for the present.

> "Please acknowledge.
> signed ... Colonel Commanding Namaqualand District."

As more depressing news reached Shelton from his intelligence sources the situation was becoming much clearer to him. His main concern was for the inhabitants of Concordia and the armed Town Guard which he needed in Okiep. A few hours after sending the first telegram to Concordia, Shelton sent a further communication:

"To the Officer Commanding Number 5 Company NTGB at Concordia - **April 1st** You will immediately bring in the whole of your company, arms, equipment and ammunition to O'OKiep by marching. Detain train to bring in spare ammunition which must be sent in today without fail. On no account is it to be left behind. If train has left you must bring the ammunition by horse wagon convoyed by your company. Move under strict service conditions with advance and rear guards, the former well ahead, and flanking files. Please tell Mr. Phillips, Captain Phillips has decided on family leaving for Port Nolloth tomorrow morning. Of course you will not think of moving yourself I quite understand."

Signed Shelton.

By the 3rd April the Boer net was closing fast.

At 7.30am a further communication was sent to the Deputy at Concordia from Shelton saying:

"We know of party you speak of on Concordia road. The enemy's strong patrol was no myth having been fired on by my eastern outpost as they passed and enemy fired on Piquet. I have sent spies along your road to ascertain if clear. If it is, I will send your escort back today. Regret having inconvenienced you but please understand all my actions dictated purely by military consideration and conditions. I can't tell time escort will leave as it depends on intelligence received which may take some time. Meanwhile, your operator should take some rest. Please number your wires as it is the only means I have of knowing whether they are genuine. All well here - shots exchanged twice during day with enemy but we had a quiet night. Keep me well informed of everything." Signed Shelton.

It was the last message Shelton sent to Concordia on the 3rd April having now decided to concentrate all his force in Okiep headquarters. The situation was to deteriorate even more rapidly for him as more bad news reached him.

General Smuts with Maritz, Bouwer and Van Deventer had now joined up their respective commandos swelling the experienced and hardy force to well over 2,500 men. The weather had also taken a turn for the worst, with very heavy rain falling on Okiep and the surrounding area, causing the river to run through the town in a flood. British intelligence had also reported to Shelton that one Louis Wessels of Harrismith Orange

River Colony was now in the neighbourhood of Okiep. It was this man who, with a party of Boers, guided General Smuts and his men away from a British patrol and found a way through from the Orange Free State into the Cape Colony, from where Smuts was to invade British held territory.

While General Smuts was concentrating his commandos for an attack on the Copper mining towns, Colonel Shelton issued defence orders to all in his garrison. These would be distributed daily during operations. He was still concerned for the fate of Concordia and with this in mind sent another telegram to his deputy there:

> "Presume all is well with you, as you give me no news. All well here. We fired on a Boer picquet 1,000 yards from one of the southern blockhouses at 1.30pm yesterday without return fire. Nababeep looted yesterday. All trains through Port Nolloth safely. The Boer troops are now encircling the mining area and are in force at Keroom 45 miles south-west of O'OKiep. From information received by me enemy is all round you. You say you have only nine days provisions whereas I clearly understood you to say you could hold out for three weeks or a month. Under these circumstances I shall be held responsible for rifles and ammunition retained by your Town Guard Battalion. This is in direct disobedience of orders received from me ordering the detachment of NTGB to join HQ of unit in O'Okiep while the road was open. Please understand I SHALL HOLD YOU DIRECTLY RESPONSIBLE IF ANY ARMS, AMMUNITION OR DYNAMITE FALLS INTO THE HANDS OF ENEMY. If it is impossible for you to smuggle arms and ammunition through here. You should retain a certain amount of dynamite and destroy all your arms and ammunition if in danger of capture. You should send every refugee you can to Steinkopf. Please acknowledge." Signed Shelton.

During that day, 4th April 1902, the situation became worse. Shelton, having received no acknowledgement to his previous wire sent another communication to Captain Phillips.

"Most Urgent to Captain Phillips, Concordia

> "After your professions and promise that you would defend the place to death on which condition you obtained a concession you requested of me to retain your arms and ammunition to enable you to do so, you now ask me whether I advise you to surrender without firing a shot. I am surprised you should address such a request to me. My answer is that so long as a round of ammunition and a man with a rifle to fire it exists, my instructions to all officers commanding posts are to hold them to the last. The onus of surrender to the enemy, whose strength you do not state, will rest with and upon you entirely and I decline in any way to be a party to it." Signed W. Shelton

By 4.00pm on the 4th April, General Smuts' commando, strength about 500 men, moved in to surround Concordia. It was at this time that Shelton had managed to get his last order through to Phillips, and again he stressed the vital importance that weapons and ammunition should not, at any cost, fall into Boer hands. Shelton made his last desperate plea: "My sole order is on no account allow arms, etc. ... make every man smash his rifle and destroy your ammunition." It was too late. At 4.45pm after being called upon to surrender by Smuts' men, Captain Phillips surrendered the town of Concordia without firing a single shot, with the result that 150 rifles, 22,000 rounds of small arms ammunition and a large quantity of dynamite were virtually given to the enemy. The surrender of Concordia was later described by one of Lord Kitchener's officers as the most disgraceful affair of the entire war. However, it must be said that there were many women and children in the town and Captain Phillips may well have thought of these non-combatants who were peaceful Namaqualanders caught up in this unnecessary war. Nevertheless, his action was to bring greater hardships to Okiep and its garrison, and all civilian inhabitants, which now included many women and children who had gathered there from Nababeep. For Colonel Shelton the news of Concordia's surrender was a bitter blow and meant that the valuable copper mines and property in Okiep were now completely isolated with no communications and little chance of the requested relief force arriving in time from Port Nolloth. The situation was indeed very grave for Okiep.

Filling a Maxim belt under the watchful eye of the sergeant

The siege of Okiep was about to begin - and with it the beginning of military operations involving almost all the principal Boer Leaders who were under the direct command of General Jan C. Smuts. Colonel Shelton's preparations for the defence of Okiep and the railway line to Port Nolloth were now going to be put to the test. He wasted little time in calling an urgent meeting with all his officers and senior NCO's to discuss the defence of the town.

The outlying blockhouses and barbed wire entanglements were put under the immediate command of Major Edwards, an Australian and Acting Staff Officer to the CO who was to be supported by the soldiers of the 5th Battalion Royal Warwickshire Regiment. The interior line of defence was to be commanded by Major Dean who was in charge of the Namaqualand Town Guard Battalion, all volunteers and semi-trained men. The entire garrison was now ordered to 'Stand to Arms'. Shelton needed time to think quietly on his own and it is recorded that he returned to his office where he sat down, filled the bowl of his pipe with tobacco, lit it, and with the dignified grace of a Victorian father, pondered the situation. He knew now that he had to make a stand against Smuts and was determined to defend his Headquarters and all the mining town to the 'bitter end'.

Shelton was from an old British military family. He had been trained at the Royal Military College Sandhurst, the finest military academy in the world, he had served in India and on the Fenian raids in Canada and had much experience as a soldier. He was not inclined to surrender one square inch of the mining properties to Smuts, but his main concern was for the women and children in Okiep.

CHAPTER 8

OKIEP 'STANDS TO ARMS' - THE SIEGE BEGINS

As the Okiep garrison waited for the attack by General Smuts and his commando force, now situated in the hills to the east and west of the town, Captain Freeland, in charge of the nine pounder field gun and the two Maxims machine guns stood to, awaiting orders to open fire. The guns were already strategically placed in position for defence. These three weapons gave Shelton considerable fire power against the greater force of Boer troops who were about to attack. Captain Borchards of the Cape Garrison Artillery was in charge of Fort Shelton, the main fortress, which was situated on a high mound (koppie) and dominated the approach to the town from the eastern ridges. This Fort formed part of Shelton's second line of defence. The Crow's Nest blockhouse was also an important link in the defence system, as was the north blockhouse, located north of Okiep on the railway line.

The St. Helena blockhouse, north-west of the railway, covered any advance by the Boers from this direction. To the south the Range blockhouse guarded the area. In all, Shelton had 13 forts located around the town and was in telephone communication with them all. Additionally, he had native runners who could carry messages should his lines be cut. His main intelligence agent was Billy Cook who knew the district well. Shelton had already made plans to counter a major Boer attack or siege which included suspension of all civil work. This meant that all mining ceased with the exception of the pumping of water. All lights were to be extinguished in the town between 7pm and 7am. Rationing of food was essential and this involved the immediate introduction of a systematic method of distribution for men, women and children and all the native population. A food committee was set up with J.B. Van Renen, Civil Commissioner and Resident Magistrate, as secretary. He was also responsible for all refugees who might arrive in the town from the more unfortunate settlements. The Headquarters of the Civil Commissioner of Namaqualand was transferred, on a temporary basis, from Springbokfontein to Okiep.

An adequate water supply was of vital importance, and fortunately Colonel Shelton was able to obtain it from four sources - (a) The mine water which flowed into the mines from copper ore bearing strata and was pumped to the surface and into the mine reservoir. It was not really suitable for drinking water unless it was boiled; (b) The water from underground for domestic purposes - this flowed into the mine from a strata of quartz and was practically pure, as extreme care was taken to prevent contamination either above or below ground. It was mixed with water of the (a) class and was also pumped through pipes to a hydrant which formed the principle water supply. As an additional precaution the water was passed through a pasteur filter. The quantity of (a) water could not be increased but the supply of (b) water could for about three months; (c) Water from Groen Kloof - an auxiliary supply which could not be relied on in the dry season. This was collected in pits about a mile from Okiep and conveyed to the town in pipes by gravitation. Shelton did not take this into consideration as the pipes could easily be cut by an attacking force and (d) Rain water - this was not normally drunk as it contained sulphur deposited on the roofs by smoke from the smelting works. The average rainfall in a month was only 1.29 inches.

Colonel Shelton ordered a daily report from the Officer Commanding the exterior lines of defence detailing all events and action. While all troops in Okiep were standing to arms he issued an emergency order to enrol additional volunteers for at least two hours drill per day - any able man from 16 years to 60 was acceptable.

While all this was taking place in Okiep, General Smuts had deployed his men among the hills overlooking the mining centre. Encouraged by his previous victories, he decided to send in a 'surrender' request to the Officer Commanding the British Garrison. At sunrise on the morning of the 5th April 1902 Deneys Reitz and P. Muller were ordered to take the letter in under a flag of truce, and as they rode up to the British soldiers at the exterior line of defence, they took note of the formidable defence system. Unfortunately, the two Boer emissaries had a somewhat hostile reception from the Royal Warwicks, whose feelings were running high following the recent news of the isolation of the town and the disgraceful surrender of Concordia. The two Boers were blindfolded and ordered to dismount. They were escorted to a tent inside the defences and told to wait for Colonel Shelton's reply to Smuts' letter.

The Surrender letter from General Smuts was taken to Colonel Shelton who read the contents, shown here in full. This was the first of three important and hitherto unpublished letters from General Smuts.

"The Officer Commanding, O'OKiep

Sir,

"If you are willing to surrender the town and the Mine properties of O'OKiep to me voluntarily and without force of arms, then on my part I am prepared to guarantee that no harm damage will be done to Mine or private property, that all lives will be spared, and that only war stores and military requirements will be taken by me - in case such belong to private individuals receipts for everything taken will be given.

"In case however I am compelled to take the place by force I reserve for myself complete freedom to deal with the above mentioned cases.

"I need not inform you that Namaqualand has all along been used as a base by the British Military Authorities from which to attack me in the rear, and you will understand that I have every reason to make an end to this state of affairs once for all. I am determined to take O'OKiep at any cost, and in case such has to be done with force it will be my sad duty to make an end of this place by totally destroying the mines and the mining properties. Such will be a military necessity in order in this way to prevent the future use of O'OKiep as a military base. In case, however, of a voluntary surrender, I shall desist herefrom.

"You are yourself aware that there is no chance of a relieving force coming to your assistance, and that I have a sufficient force to take O'OKiep, and as I conceive that your especial object is to protect the mining properties I hope that you will recognise the reasonableness of accepting my proposal.

"I shall be glad to have a speedy answer hereto.

"If you think it necessary I am willing to have an interview with you today between our lines.

"I have the honour etc.
(signed) J.C. Smuts, Asst Commdt Genl

"Concordia
5.4.1902

"P.S. Under same cover please find a letter for Mrs Dorrington from her husband. Please hand same to her."

(Stamped -   District Office
                      No 3456
                      Apr. 5 1902
                      O'OKiep Namaqualand)

After much thought Colonel Shelton dictated his diplomatic reply to General Smuts:

"Reply no 1   (Stamped -   District Office
                                        No 3456
                                        Apr. 5 1902
                                        O'OKiep Namaqualand)
"Asst. Commandant General Smuts
Concordia

Sir,

"I have the honour to acknowledge receipt of your letter of today's date & regret delay in replying to it caused by my being from my Head Quarters when it arrived.

"In reply I beg to inform you O'OKiep is a fortified town & that I am comfortably supplied with men, ammunition and provisions.

"You are correct in your inference that my Duty is to protect and defend the mining property etc, and I may add that it is my intention to act with that object - As an Imperial Officer I am not in a position to make terms of any kind - I have to acknowledge with thanks your courtesy in sending in Mrs Dorrington's letter from her husband - It may obviate trouble &

misunderstanding if I state at once that I must decline further correspondence on this subject.

"I have the honour to be
Sir
Your Obedient Servant
W. Shelton Lieutenant Colonel
Commanding Namaqualand District."

The letter was then handed to Reitz and his friend Muller who, still blindfolded, were helped to remount their horses for the short trip back to their lines. They were then led to the outer defence area where the blindfolds were removed and they rode off towards Concordia to deliver Shelton's reply to General Smuts.

As the Boers galloped away Shelton sent word to all at the outer and inner defences to stand by for immediate action. This was not long in coming, in fact, shortly after General Smuts had read Shelton's reply, he ordered a force of his troops to attack Okiep. His men opened fire at a range of over 1,000 yards from the eastern hills overlooking the town and this rapidly cleared the parade ground where a small group of soldiers were standing. The Okiep defences replied with heavy fire.

Okiep was now under a fierce attack and as the defensive fire intensified, General Smuts and his men began to realize that the capture of the town was not going to be easy. Nevertheless, the general situation on April 6th was by no means favourable for the garrison. Further along the railway line the Boers had begun destroying parts of the track and had blown up two culverts near Anenous. General Smuts had established his headquarters in a large house in Concordia. On the railway line, the last train had arrived at Okiep from Port Nolloth at 4pm on the 4th April and there was no other movement to and from the outside world. However, Shelton's particular concern was for the two very important wooden viaducts at Anenous just west of Klipfontein which were being defended by the 2nd Battalion of the Namaqualand Border Scouts under the command of Lieutenants Meyrick and Moffat. Lieutenant Moffat was also the Railway Traffic Manager for the Cape Copper Company. The railway link was vitally important and had to be protected at all costs since it was the only direct route for Shelton's supplies from Port Nolloth. On the 6th April Shelton had received via his scout Billy Cook a message from Lieutenant Meyrick reporting that 50 Boers, under a white flag, had demanded the surrender of the blockhouse at Ratelpoort. This has been rejected.

Colonel Shelton remained calm as he considered what General Smuts' next move was likely to be. He was determined to defend Okiep at any cost - and the civilian population was solidly behind him and prepared to use every means available. The main danger was at night when the enemy could advance on the blockhouses undetected. As the Boers were in the hills overlooking the town, the Royal Warwicks adjusted their sights in order to engage the eastern and western ridges and the unseen enemy. Shelton's nine pounder field gun had not, up to this point, been in action, and Captain Freeland RA was also holding the two Maxims machine guns in readiness. The Boers opened up a heavy and concentrated fire from their positions on the high ground.

The Officer Commanding,
        O'okiep.

Sir,

        If you are willing to surrender
the town and the mine properties
of O'okiep to me voluntarily and
without force of arms, then on
my part I am prepared to guarantee that no ~~harm~~ damage
will be done to mine or private
property, that all lives will be
spared, ~~so~~ and that only war stores
and military requirements will be
taken by me - in case such belong
to private individuals receipts
for everything taken will be given.
        In case however I am com-
pelled to take the place by force
I reserve for myself complete
freedom to deal with the above
mentioned cases.
        I need not inform you that
Namaqualand has all along been
used as a base by the British
Military Authorities from which
to attack me in the rear,

Page 1 of General Smuts' letter dated 5th April 1902 to Colonel Shelton

111

and you will understand that I have every reason to make an end to this state of affairs once for all. I am determined to take O'okiep at any cost, and in case such has to be done with force it will be my sad duty to make an end of this place by totally destroying the mines and the mining properties. Such will be a military necessity in order in this way to prevent the future use of O'okiep as a military base. In case however of a voluntary surrender I shall desist herefrom.

You are yourself aware that there is no chance of a relieving force coming to your assistance, and that I have a sufficient force to take O'okiep, and as I conceive that your especial object is to protect the mining properties I hope that you will recognise the reasonableness of accepting my proposal.

I shall be glad to have a speedy answer hereto.

If you think it necessary I am willing to have an interview with

Page 2 of Smuts' letter to Shelton

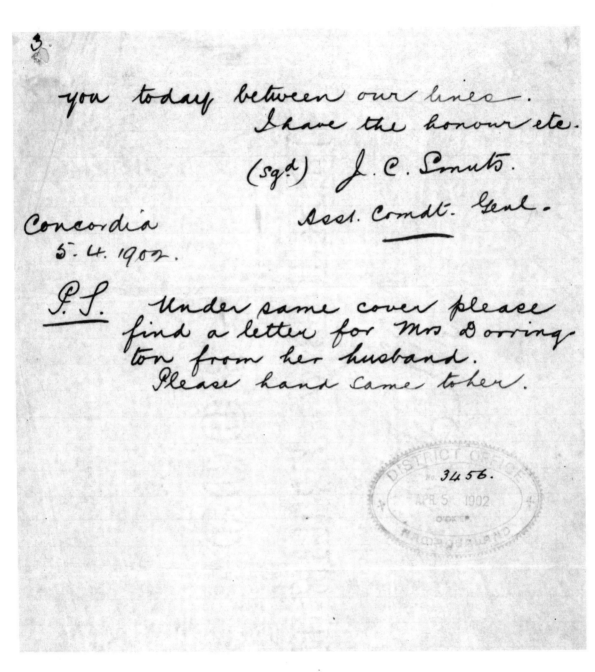

you today between our lines —.

I have the honour etc.

(sgd) J. C. Smuts.

Asst. Comdt. Genl.

Concordia
5. 4. 1902.

P.S.   Under same cover please find a letter for Mrs Dorrington from her husband.
Please hand same to her.

3456.

APR 5 1902

Page 3 of Smuts' letter to Shelton

Reply No 1

Asst. Commandant General Smuts

Concordia

Sir,

I have the honour to acknowledge receipt of your letter of todays date, & regret delay in replying to it caused by my being away from my Head Quarters when it arrived.

In reply I beg to inform you O'OKIEP is a fortified town & that I am comfortably supplied with Men, Ammunition and provisions.

You are correct in your inference that My Duty is to protect and defend the mining property etc, and I may add that it is my intention to act with that object, - As an Imperial Officer I am not in a position to make terms of any kind, - I have to acknowledge with thanks your courtesy in sending in Mrs Dorrington's letter from her husband, - It may obviate trouble & misunderstanding if I state at once that I must decline further correspondence on this subject

I have the honour to be

Sir

Your Obedient Servant,

Commanding. Namaqualand District.

Colonel Shelton's reply dated 5th April 1902 to General Smuts's letter

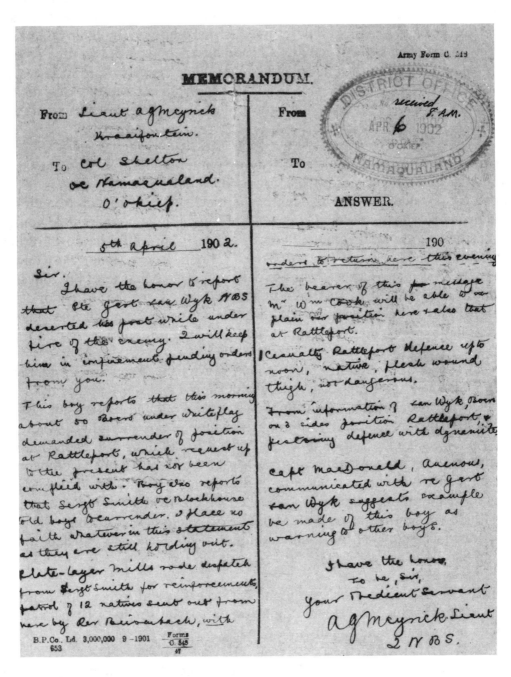

Memorandum from Meyrick to Col. Shelton. April 6th 1902.

Private Carolus Johannes, a coloured man of the Namaqualand Town Guard Battalion, was the first casualty of the Okiep garrison. While reloading his Martini-Henry rifle he was hit by four Mauser bullets in the head, chest and stomach. He was dragged back under cover by a Warwick soldier and at the same time three other members of the exterior defences were wounded, two seriously. The Boer shooting was, as always, deadly accurate for they had been carefully trained as sharpshooters by their fathers from an early age. During this siege of Shelton's headquarters he had drawn up a record of all members of his garrison, which included Colonel White's men cut off at Garies, his men at Port Nolloth and at Anenous on the railway and had added up the arms and animals in his command. The three pages of his Field State show the manpower situation on 7th April 1902.

At 2pm on the 8th April the Boers attacked the southern blockhouses and began a heavy fire from the eastern ridges into the town. Colonel Shelton, who was in constant telephone communication with his men in the blockhouses, directed the defence from his headquarters. Captain Freeland opened fire with his nine pounder field gun, shelling enemy positions. Meanwhile, along the railway line 12 miles to the north of the town, the blockhouse at Ratelpoort was attacked by Boers troops under the command of General Van Deventer. This was repulsed after a fierce exchange of fire, but the Boers had withdrawn in order to obtain dynamite with which to force the surrender of the little outpost. However, unknown to them, while they were away, the blockhouse was evacuated; the men reaching Steinkopf safely later that afternoon.

On the railway to Port Nolloth, Shelton had previously issued orders to Lieutenant Moffat and his men to evacuate the railway blockhouse and retire upon Jules Hoogte to defend the water works there which supplied Port Nolloth and its garrison. Billy Cook, had made his way through the Boer lines at Kraaifontein on the railway where his task was to stop a train loaded with supplies and save it from falling into enemy hands. The locomotive and its carriages were the property of the Cape Copper Company and his quick action saved the train from certain destruction. Shelton had now placed the garrison on siege rations which was controlled by the food supply committee, and he recorded his food supplies as on 26th March 1902. Note his comments: "This was the extent of our food supply at the commencement of the Siege of O'OKiep, but instead of feeding 800 I had to feed 6,000."

Captain Borchards, the garrison's Adjutant, was to act as staff officer to Shelton during the siege, with Captain MacDonald employed on special service. It was necessary to issue siege notes for people to purchase goods.

Okiep was now very well organised to withstand the Boer attack and to resist any attempts to capture the town and the valuable mining property. While the garrison troops kept up the return fire from the outer defence area, General Smuts had decided to use dynamite bombs against the blockhouses which were being successful in keeping his men pinned down. The surrender of the Concordia mine had given the Boers access to a large quantity of dynamite and fuses, and after his success at Springbokfontein, Smuts decided to subject the Okiep defences to the same treatment. As night fell it brought with it more danger for the garrison, as Shelton had realized the enemy would make determined efforts to advance close enough to throw dynamite bombs onto the

*Generals Smuts, Jaap Van Deventer and Manie Maritz
outside O'OKiep, April 1902.*

General Smuts and his faithful horse "Charlie" shot by a British patrol.

117

FIELD STATE.
I.

Army Form B. 239 (Special).

Place Namaqualand District. Date 7th April, 1902.

Unit.		At Hd. Qrs. Officers	At Hd. Qrs. Other Ranks	On Det. Officers	On Det. Other Ranks	Total. Officers	Total. Other Ranks	Sick Officers	Sick Other Ranks	Horses	Mules	Oxen	Guns Field	Guns Position	Guns Howitzers		Remarks.
O'Okiep	District Staff	6	16			6	16			6			Brigade in OOKIEP.				O.C.District. Maj Edwards...
Port Nolloth	2nd Nam. Border Scouts	1	3			1	3										
	Nam. Town Guard Batt.	3	130			3	130										
Amenous	1st Nam. Border Scouts		9				9		4				defending PORTNOLLOTH.				
	2nd do. do. do.	2	54			2	54										
	Cape Gar. Artillery		25				25	1						1		2	
O'Okiep	5th Royal Warwick Regt.	3	47			3	47										
Hd. Qrs. of District.	1st Nam. Border Scouts	2	70			2	70	1	35	1			Besieged in OOKIEP.				
	Nam. Town Guard Batt.	16	511			16	511										
	Medical		1				1										
	Carried Forward	34	865			34	865	2	45	1				1		2	

(Signed)

Commanding

INSTRUCTIONS.

1. Field States will be made up corrected to Mondays, inclusive, and will be forwarded every week to the Chief Staff Officer of your District as soon after as possible.
2. Care must be taken to state the nature (or calibre) of guns—e.g. 15 Pr. B.L., 2·5 Inch R.M.L., 4·7 Inch Q.F., ·303 Maxims, &c.
3. The number of Officers and Other Ranks, &c., on the Station Staff must be included as a separate unit.
4. No other form of Field State except this to be rendered.
5. All arrivals and departures of troops affecting this return to be reported by telegraph, or other quickest means, giving exact details as to numbers, date of arrival or departure, and destination, &c., by cypher or in clear as occasion demands.
6. On the back of the return give station and strength of each Detachment.

Field State page one - "The last Field State rendered during Siege of O'OKiep". W. Shelton.

118

FIELD STATE.

Army Form B. 239 (Special).

HWV 25,000 8—01
4 13 52

Place _Namaqualand District_   Date _7th April, 1902_

Unit.	Fit for duty. At Hd. Qrs. Officers	Other Ranks	On Det. Officers	Other Ranks	Total. Officers	Other Ranks	Sick at Hd. Qrs. or Det. Officers	Other Ranks	Animals. Horses	Mules	Oxen	Vehicles. Buckwagons	Scotch Carts	Water Carts	S.A.A. Carts	Arty. or G.S. Wagons	Natives	Guns. Field	Position	Howitzers	Machine	Remarks.
Brought forward	34	865			34	865	2		45	1								1			2	
Transport									4	(10)	242	(49)	2	1								all mule transport at GARIES. Capt. W. Mitchell I.S.H.L.C.I.
Remounts									75							16						Capt. A.D. Freeland. no. R.D. 25 Pts. 20 Sick. including No. 2
Intelligence	1	11			1	11			7							60						P. Mch. II. Macbeth, Int. Agent.
Cape Garr. Artillery	6				6																	
3rd Garrison R.W. Surrey (?)	4				4																	Colonel White
1st Nam. Border Scouts	1	69			1	69			42									Colonel White's Column shut up in GARIES				Capt. E.H. Hodges R.A.S.
2nd do. do. do.		86				86												since 20/3/02.				
Nam. Town Guard Batt.	1	22			1	22																
Carried forward.	37	1063			37	1063	2		189	151	242	39	2	1		76		1			2	

(Signed)

Commanding _____

INSTRUCTIONS.

1. Field States will be made up corrected to Mondays, inclusive, and will be forwarded every week to the Chief Staff Officer of your District as soon after as possible.
2. Care must be taken to state the nature (or calibre) of guns—e.g., 15 Pr. B.L., 2·5 Inch R.M.L., 4·7 Inch Q.F., ·303 Maxims, &c.
3. The number of Officers and Other Ranks, &c., on the Station Staff must be included as a separate unit.
4. No other form of Field State except this to be rendered.
5. All arrivals and departures of troops affecting this return to be reported by telegraph, or other quickest means, giving exact details as to numbers, date of arrival or departure, and destination, &c., by cypher or in clear as occasion demands.
6. On the back of the return give station and strength of each Detachment.

Field State page two.

FIELD STATE.

Army Form B. 239 (Special).

HWV 25,000 8—01
4 13 52

Place _Namaqualand District_   Date _7th April, 1902_

Unit.	Fit for duty. At Hd. Qrs. Officers	Other Ranks	On Det. Officers	Other Ranks	Total. Officers	Other Ranks	Sick at Hd. Qrs. or Det. Officers	Other Ranks	Animals. Horses	Mules	Oxen	Vehicles. Buckwagons	Scotch Carts	Water Carts	S.A.A. Carts	Arty. or G.S. Wagons	Natives	Guns. Field	Position	Howitzers	Machine	Remarks.
Brought forward	57	1063			57	1063	2		189	151	242	39	2	1		76		1			2	
Staff	3	2			3	2			6													O.C. Column 5.0, m.o. Col. White R.A.
Cape Garr. Artillery	2	26			2	26			29								1	shut up in GARIES since 20/3/02.				
5th Royal Warwick Regt.	2	26			2	26			30													
1st Nam. Border Scouts	4	234			4	234			225	29												
Intelligence		1				1			23								21					
Total.	48	1352			48	1352	2		502	210	242	39	2	1		97		2			2	
Missing & Prisoners.																						Casualties
1st N.B.S. + 2 N.B.S.Coy. Jnc. Matufeyke Ret.		3	17						36	4												11 Killed 13 Wounded.
Town Guard 12 N.B.S.		3	106																			Nil.

(Signed) _W. Shelton Lt. Colonel._

Commanding _Defence Force. O'OKIEP._

INSTRUCTIONS.

1. Field States will be made up corrected to Mondays, inclusive, and will be forwarded every week to the Chief Staff Officer of your District as soon after as possible.
2. Care must be taken to state the nature (or calibre) of guns—e.g., 15 Pr. B.L., 2·5 Inch R.M.L., 4·7 Inch Q.F., ·303 Maxims, &c.
3. The number of Officers and Other Ranks, &c., on the Station Staff must be included as a separate unit.
4. No other form of Field State except this to be rendered.
5. All arrivals and departures of troops affecting this return to be reported by telegraph, or other quickest means, giving exact details as to numbers, date of arrival or departure, and destination, &c., by cypher or in clear as occasion demands.
6. On the back of the return give station and strength of each Detachment.

Field State page three. Signed W. Shelton Lt.Colonel
Commanding Defence Force. O'OKiep.

119

NAMAQUALAND FIELD FORCE

Feeding strength

MEN_____301

HORSES_____566

MULES_____211

District Office stamp:
DISTRICT OFFICE
No.
MAR 25 1902
O'OKIEP.
NAMAQUALAND

SUPPLIES	DAYS	RATIONED TO.
Biscuits & Flour	188	29th.September 1902
Preserved Meat etc.	150	22nd.August 1902
Tea Coffee etc.	578	24th.October 1903
Sugar	123	26th.July 1902
Salt & Pepper	762	26th.April 1904
Compressed Vegetables	380	12th.April 1903

Emergency Rations(1597 tins)

FORAGE

Hay etc.	65	29th.May 1902
Oats etc.	114	17th.July 1902

-:-:-:-:-:-:-:-:-:-:-:-:-:-:-:-:-

*This was the extent of our food supply
at the commencement of the siege of O'OKiEP.
but instead of feeding 800 shed to feed 6000.*

W. Shelton.

Lieut.-Colonel,
Commandg. Namaqualand District.

District Office stamp:
DISTRICT OFFICE
No.
JUN 6 1902
O'OKIEP.
NAMAQUALAND

Copy of Shelton's food supplies at commencement of Siege of O'OKiep.

120

At O'okiep, April 1902

1. Field Cornet C. Brink   2. Commandant B. D. Bouwer   3. Field Cornet A. G. Boshoff   4. General J. L. van Deventer   5. B. D. Bouwer Senior   6. General J. C. Smuts   7. Field Cornet W. Kotzé   8. Corporal H. Vermaas   9. General S. G. Maritz   10. Field Cornet J. van Brummelen   11. Commandant S. Schoeman   12. J. Brink   13. Field Cornet A. Standers   14. Field Cornet J. van den Berg   15. Field Cornet P. F. Visser   16. C. T. Möller   17. Marquis Robert de Kersauson   18. Field Cornet B. Coetzee.

A group of Boer leaders with General Smuts at Okiep
By courtesy of W. Hancock Esg

121

blockhouse roofs. He had ordered all picquets to withdraw from the outer line of defence to within the second line, with the exception of the number one Range Kloof and Concordia picquets. He considered that after nightfall the other members of the blockhouses should be evacuated until dawn, when the observation post manned by his intelligence scouts reported Boer movement. Fort Shelton blockhouse, the main stronghold of the town's inner defence system was manned at night and defended by troops of the Namaqualand Town Guard Battalion in trenches. Major Edwards had gathered a strong reserve of 50 men to guard the entire area at night.

At 11.15pm on the 9th April, a dark night, the Boers crept up silently towards the Crow's Nest (the blockhouse on raised ground near Fort Shelton) and the Shelton blockhouse. There were about 20 men in the assault party and as they neared the first fort someone trod on a twig and the sound gave their position away to the watchful sentries who immediately challenged the darkness beyond. The answer, in the form of dynamite grenades, was quick in coming. The first landed so near to the blockhouse that it brought down a side of the structure with a resounding crash and blew dust and pieces of mortar in all directions. Two bombs fell short of their target with a terrifying explosion which stunned the occupants inside the fort who, on recovering, thought the Boers had a field gun. The sudden noise alerted the entire defence system which quickly opened fire into the darkness. The Crow's Nest continued a heavy fire until 12.50am when the Boers threw two more bombs onto the blockhouse roof, causing more shock and confusion. The Boers then rushed the dazed defenders taking nearly all of them prisoners, but in the darkness and mêlée that followed three native scouts managed to escape to Fort Shelton with their rifles and ammunition. The other less fortunate men were then taken away towards the enemy's lines.

The Crow's Nest blockhouse was garrisoned by one white intelligence scout who was in charge of fifteen natives of the Namaqualand Town Guard. The Boers had forced the Crow's Nest blockhouse to surrender after using eight dynamite bombs against it, and it had put up a stiff resistance despite the unexpected nature of the attack. Two men had managed to escape to the north blockhouse where Lieutenant Anstey sent one back to the town to report that he has lost his troop. The other man went with Captain Jones to the Concordia blockhouse to help in the removal of stores. The three native scouts who had succeeded in withdrawing to Fort Shelton blockhouse with their rifles and some ammunition were to reinforce its garrison. Major Edwards, who was in charge of the outer defences, sent a native runner with a note to intelligence agent Robinson who was to take it to Colonel Shelton with a full report on the loss of the Crow's Nest. The report stated briefly that one white intelligence scout was missing and that three natives and 7 NTG scouts were returning to camp with rifles and ammunition.

The surrender of the Crow's Nest was the first bitter blow to the garrison. Shelton was concerned about the use of dynamite grenades as reports had already reached him that the women and children in the town were very frightened by the large explosions on the Crow's Nest. After the surrender of the Crow's Nest, Shelton ordered 12 men to join Major Edwards in the outer defences taking extra ammunition. Accordingly, a message was sent by Captain Borchards to warn Edwards that Sergeant Clacker and his men would approach him from the direction of the English Church.

On His Majesty's Service.

10s.   O'OKIEP SIEGE NOTE.   10s.

May, 1902.   -------------------   May, 1902.

This Note is Good for

TEN SHILLINGS

No. *597.*   (STERLING).   No. *597.*

and will be exchanged for coin on 31st May, 1902
at the Office of Administrator, NAMAQUALAND at O'OKIEP

Issued by Authority of Lieut:Colonel W. A. D. Shelton,
Administrator, NAMAQUALAND DISTRICT.

G.K.K.Macdonald Captain.   *W. J. Wood* Lieut.

Staff Officer to Administrator.   Paymaster, Namaqualand.

NOTE. This note is not negotiable unless signed by both Staff Officer
and Paymaster.

*A rare Siege Note. Capt. Borcherds, the Garrison's Adjudant was to
act as staff officers to Shelton during the siege, with Capt. MacDonald,
employed on special service. It was necessary to issue Siege Notes for
people to purchase goods.*

The attack on the Shelton blockhouse was unsuccessful on this occasion, but the Boers had contented themselves with one surrender and withdrew back to the hills, leaving a few of their men in the abandoned Crow's Nest for observation. The Boers had managed for the first time to penetrate the outer defences and advanced close enough to throw their dynamite grenades at Fort Shelton itself, but these had little effect on the main stronghold of the headquarters. At 2.10am there was a terrific explosion which shook the town and echoed around the hills. At first Colonel Shelton thought Fort Shelton had been blown up, but this was not the case. The few bombs which the remaining Boers threw at the Fort landed short and exploded harmlessly on open ground.

The garrison responded with heavy fire which compelled the Boers to withdraw to their positions in the hills. After a short lull until 4.30am, another party of Boers returned to attack Concordia blockhouse but the garrison was ready for them. The assault was repulsed and the firing ceased at 5am. At 6am the officer commanding the Concordia blockhouse reported that the enemy had evacuated the Crow's Nest after a heavy fire had been directed into it by his men. As the Boers passed his outpost the officer expected an attack, but this did not happen. He continued firing as they withdrew not knowing if anyone had been hit, but on hearing groans and curses coming from the Boers, his men realized they had inflicted some punishment on the attackers.

Later that day Colonel Shelton issued a notice to all the garrison and civilian population, praising the coolness and steadiness displayed by Major Edwards and his men of Fort Shelton under not only heavy rifle fire, but dynamite attack. He continued: "The experience gained from last night's action is that the bark of the latter is worse than its bite, and that the troops have little to fear from dynamite bombs being thrown, as the enemy is doing - providing the men pour a hot fire on them as did Fort Shelton. "Every effort," he said, "should be made to prevent the enemy getting inside the barbed wire and near to the blockhouses to project the bombs".

During that night the Boers had succeeded in cutting the tangled barbed wire of the outer defences, but the fire from the other blockhouses and defensive positions was so hot that they were not able to penetrate in numbers beyond that line. Major Edwards' defence of Fort Shelton, supported by the NCO's and men under his command, was a fine example and would encourage the defenders of the town to act accordingly when their turn came.

Two women who were taking water to the troops in the inner trenches, were hit by Boer fire from the eastern ridges, and badly wounded. Their screams brought medical orderlies to attend to them and one of them was deliberately fired upon but luckily not hit. Doctor Howard, the only Medical Officer of the garrison was working around the clock assisted by various ladies in the hospital, and medical orderlies who attended to the casualties.

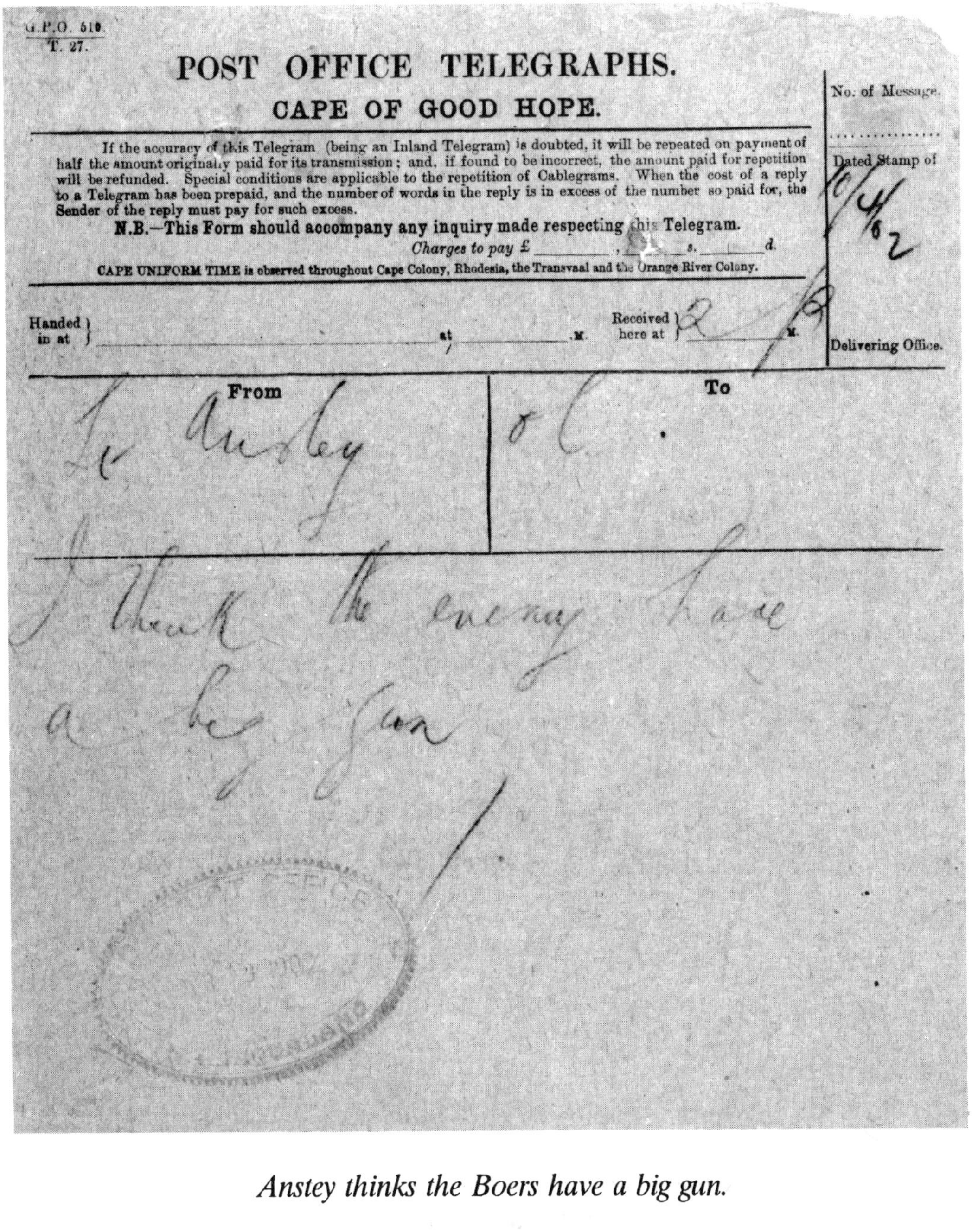

G.P.O. 510.
T. 27.

POST OFFICE TELEGRAPHS.

CAPE OF GOOD HOPE.

If the accuracy of this Telegram (being an Inland Telegram) is doubted, it will be repeated on payment of half the amount originally paid for its transmission; and, if found to be incorrect, the amount paid for repetition will be refunded. Special conditions are applicable to the repetition of Cablegrams. When the cost of a reply to a Telegram has been prepaid, and the number of words in the reply is in excess of the number so paid for, the Sender of the reply must pay for such excess.

N.B.—This Form should accompany any inquiry made respecting this Telegram.

Charges to pay £ ____ s. ____ d.

CAPE UNIFORM TIME is observed throughout Cape Colony, Rhodesia, the Transvaal and the Orange River Colony.

No. of Message.

Dated Stamp of 10/4/02

Handed in at ____ at ____ M. Received here at 2 P. M.

Delivering Office.

From	To
To Anstey	O C

I think the enemy have a big gun

Anstey thinks the Boers have a big gun.

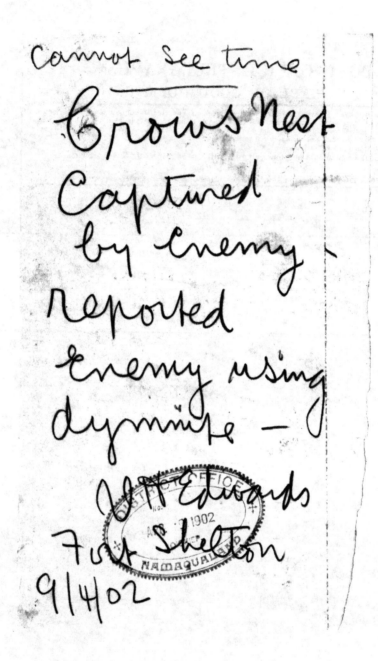

cannot see time

Crows Nest
Captured
by Enemy -
reported
Enemy using
dynamite -

J.H. Edwards
Fort Shelton
9/4/02

*Crow's Nest captured - enemy reported
using dynamite*

Anstey reports Boers attacking Fort Shelton and believes they have something which will throw dynamite for a considerable distance. 10 April, 1902.

POST OFFICE TELEGRAPHS.
CAPE OF GOOD HOPE.

No. of Message.

If the accuracy of this Telegram (being an Inland Telegram) is doubted, it will be repeated on payment of half the amount originally paid for its transmission; and, if found to be incorrect, the amount paid for repetition will be refunded. Special conditions are applicable to the repetition of Cablegrams. When the cost of a reply to a Telegram has been prepaid, and the number of words in the reply is in excess of the number so paid for, the Sender of the reply must pay for such excess.

N.B.—This Form should accompany any inquiry made respecting this Telegram.

Charges to pay £ _____ ,, _____ s. _____ d.

CAPE UNIFORM TIME is observed throughout Cape Colony, Rhodesia, the Transvaal and the Orange River Colony.

Dated Stamp of

Handed in _____ at _____ .M.   Received here at _____ .M.

Delivering Office.

From   Lt Ansley   O   To

The enemy are blasting around the Crows Nest and are crossing the plain You had better send out reinforcements
11/16   7 mi a pm

Urgent message from Lt Anstey re Dynamite Bombs around Crow's Nest

128

POST OFFICE TELEGRAPHS.

CAPE OF GOOD HOPE.

No. of Message.

. . . .

If the accuracy of this Telegram (being an Inland Telegram) is doubted, it will be repeated on payment of half the amount originally paid for its transmission; and, if found to be incorrect, the amount paid for repetition will be refunded. Special conditions are applicable to the repetition of Cablegrams. When the cost of a reply to a Telegram has been prepaid, and the number of words in the reply is in excess of the number so paid for, the Sender of the reply must pay for such excess.

Dated Stamp of

N.B.—This Form should accompany any inquiry made respecting this Telegram.

Charges to pay £ _____ ,, _____ s. _____ d.

CAPE UNIFORM TIME is observed throughout Cape Colony, Rhodesia, the Transvaal and the Orange River Colony.

Handed in at } _____ at ♦ _____ M. Received here at } _____ M.

Delivering Office.

From

To

Lt. Anstey is afraid the Crows Nest has surrendered firing ceased.

129

POST OFFICE TELEGRAPHS.

CAPE OF GOOD HOPE.

G.P.O. 510.
T. 27.

No. of Message.

If the accuracy of this Telegram (being an Inland Telegram) is doubted, it will be repeated on payment of half the amount originally paid for its transmission; and, if found to be incorrect, the amount paid for repetition will be refunded. Special conditions are applicable to the repetition of Cablegrams. When the cost of a reply to a Telegram has been prepaid, and the number of words in the reply is in excess of the number so paid for, the Sender of the reply must pay for such excess.

N.B.—This Form should accompany any inquiry made respecting this Telegram.

Charges to pay £ _____ ,, _____ s. _____ d.

CAPE UNIFORM TIME is observed throughout Cape Colony, Rhodesia, the Transvaal and the Orange River Colony.

Dated Stamp of

8/4/02

Handed in at } 1. am. at _____ M. Received here at } _____ M.

Delivering Office.

From	To
O. C.	Major Edwards

I am sending you Serjt. Clacker & Eleven men to further reinforce you. These men will approach you from the direction of the English Church. I am also sending you up six boxes of Martini Henry ammunition.

By order.

Allan Borchards Capt.
S.O.

Borchards message to Major Edwards sent at 1.am., on the 10th April, 1902.

POST OFFICE TELEGRAPHS.
CAPE OF GOOD HOPE.

No. of Message.

....

Dated Stamp of

Handed in at _____ 11 at . 10 / ... 24

Received here at _____ x.

Delivering Office.

From *Lt. Ainsley*   To *O.C. Drift*

Shell from big guns burst beautifully in the right place

Report on success of OKiep's nine pounder field gun

131

Order from Shelton to Lt. Anstey regarding vigilance in case of night attack by Boers

CHAPTER 9

NO SURRENDER TO GENERAL SMUTS

It was now the eleventh day of the siege and Colonel Shelton, although issuing a notice to advise to the garrison that the dynamite bombs were not to be feared, was becoming deeply concerned for the safety of the women and children in the town. On Thursday, 10th April, he called a general meeting of his senior officers and officials to express his anxiety. He suggested it might be desirable to approach General Smuts with the object of obtaining his agreement to evacuating the women and children to Port Nolloth. After much discussion, it was decided by a large majority that the women and children should remain and face the perils and hardships of the siege, none of them wanting to be separated from their husbands. In addition to this, the members of the meeting also rejected a proposal that a protest should be sent to General Smuts on the use of dynamite. It was resolved that no communication should be made on the subject to the enemy. "Under the circumstances then", Colonel Shelton said, "I reserve the right to follow the enemy's lead and adopt similar tactics."

He then gave a general warning that women and children should not venture out during the day time as the fire from both the eastern and western ridges was intensifying, and sniping by Boer marksmen was continuous. A 'Review of the Rations' was made, with provision for a 'rum ration' to be sent up to Fort Shelton and the outer Forts on a nightly basis. Shelton also requested an urgent return of all ammunition in the garrison so as to ascertain his reserves.

During this meeting the Boers opened fire again from the hills, and the exchange went on all day from 7.30am until 6pm that evening, with much ammunition being expended on both sides. At 4.51pm the Officer Commanding north section, Lieutenant Anstey, telephoned Shelton to tell him that a strong force of the enemy was moving across his front from east to west.

General Smuts was moving some of his troops to positions on the west side of the town to concentrate a force for further attacks after nightfall and which by now the Okiep garrison was beginning to fear. At about 8pm the Boers began another determined attack on the town, concentrating on the Shelton blockhouse. Again they had succeeded in advancing close enough to throw their dynamite bombs. Sergeant Arthur of the 5th Royal Warwicks Battalion handled the situation calmly showing a fine example to the rest of his men as he directed their fire into the advancing enemy. The intense fire was so effective in keeping the enemy at bay that no serious damage was done to the blockhouse, although the Boers achieved some success when an outer wall of the building was damaged. After about half an hour the Boers decided to withdraw and did not return that night. Okiep was fairly quiet again for a few hours.

Two other men of the garrison who showed much bravery and courage in the face of the enemy were Sergeant Peart EE, Royal Engineers and Sapper Larg, who under heavy fire from the Boers, removed unused mines from the foot of Fort Shelton.

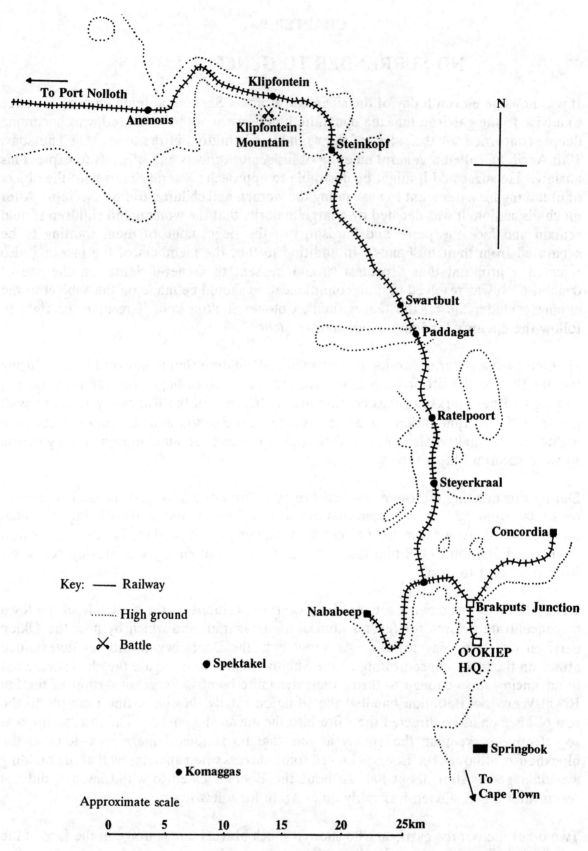

Key:
— Railway
.... High ground
✕ Battle

To Port Nolloth
Anenous
Klipfontein
Klipfontein Mountain
Steinkopf
Swartbult
Paddagat
Ratelpoort
Steyerkraal
Concordia
Nababeep
Brakputs Junction
O'OKIEP H.Q.
Spektakel
Springbok
To Cape Town
Komaggas

Approximate scale

0   5   10   15   20   25km

By courtesy of the late Henry Robert Moffatt Esq.

Map of general plan of the area covered by the Boer Forces during
the siege of O'Okiep

Map of O'Okiep showing positions of main blockhouses

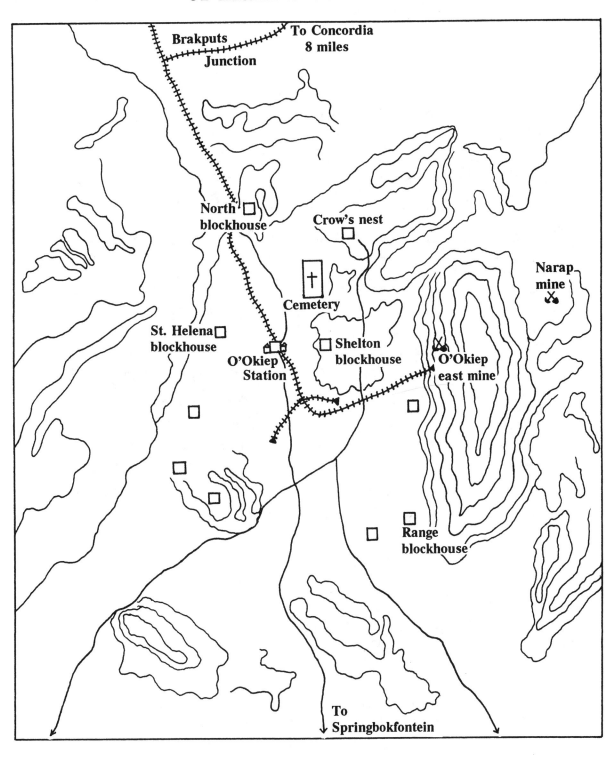

Brakputs Junction

To Concordia 8 miles

North blockhouse

Crow's nest

Narap mine

Cemetery

St. Helena blockhouse

Shelton blockhouse

O'Okiep Station

O'Okiep east mine

Range blockhouse

To Springbokfontein

☐ —— Blockhouse

⚒ —— Disused mine

++++++ —— Railway line

POST OFFICE TELEGRAPHS.
CAPE OF GOOD HOPE.

No. of Message.
....

Dated Stamp of

If the accuracy of this Telegram (being an Inland Telegram) is doubted, it will be repeated on payment of half the amount originally paid for its transmission; and, if found to be incorrect, the amount paid for repetition will be refunded. Special conditions are applicable to the repetition of Cablegrams. When the cost of a reply to a Telegram has been prepaid, and the number of words in the reply is in excess of the number so paid for, the Sender of the reply must pay for such excess.

N.B.—This Form should accompany any inquiry made respecting this Telegram.

Charges to pay £ _____ „ _____ s. _____ d.

CAPE UNIFORM TIME is observed throughout Cape Colony, Rhodesia, the Transvaal and the Orange River Colony.

Handed in at) 4.30 pm   at 6.   m.   Received here at) 4.58 p   Delivering Office.

From: Lt. Anstey

To: O.C. Operations

There is a very large body of the enemy about 2 or 3 miles to the north of north block house. The dust is very long. They are moving from east to west.

10th April 1902

W.F.S.

A large force of Boers reported moving north of the
north blockhouse. Lt. Anstey to Col. Shelton.

136

At daybreak on the following morning the Boers opened fire from the eastern ridges, and by 7.10am there was a continuous exchange of rifle fire and the garrison's nine pounder field gun also fired accurately at the Boer positions in the hills.

The fight continued until 5pm when troops manning the outer defences saw another 'White Flag of Truce' being brought in by two Boer horsemen. It was another letter from General Smuts, addressed to Colonel Shelton that proposed the removal of all non-combatants from the town to a place of safety.

> "Lieut. Colonel Shelton   District office no. 3464 TK
> O'OKiep   14D
>   April 11th, 1902
>   Namaqualand.
>
> Sir.
>
> Notwithstanding the curt manner in which you have closed all further correspondence with me in your despatch of April 5, 1902, yet for the sake of humanity I wish to propose the following. I have noticed that several houses in the town have been fortified for defensive purposes, and that non-combatants go about the town at the peril of their lives. As it my be reasonably expected so long as the civil population remains in the town, that casualties will occur among them, I would suggest that the women and children and the ambulance hospitals be removed from the town in the direction of the Springbokfontein road, so that the non-combatants may be outside the town of O'OKiep but inside the line of forts. If you are willing to make use of this suggestion I shall afford you an opportunity to-morrow (Saturday), during the day, to effect this removal, and during that time there will be an armistice between us with your consent. Thereafter I shall not hold myself responsible for any casualties among your non-combatants.
>
> I have the honour to be,
> Your obedient Servant,
> (sgn) J.C. Smuts,
> Asst. Comdt. Genl.
>
> Concordia
> 11.4.1902."

No 2

36.

Lieut:-Colonel Shelton,
    O'okiep.

Sir,
            Notwithstanding the curt
manner in which you have closed
all further correspondence with
me in your despatch of April 5,
1902, yet for the sake of humanity
I wish to propose the following.
I have noticed that several houses
in the town have been fortified
for defensive purposes, and that
non-combattants go about the town
at the peril of their lives. As
it may be reasonably expected,
so ~~sola~~ long as the civil population remains in the town,
that casualties will occur among
them, I would suggest that the
women and children and the
ambulance hospitals be removed
from the town in the direction
of the Springbokfontein road, so
that the non-combattants may
be outside the town of O'okiep but
                                inside

*Page 1 of the second letter from General Smuts dated 11th April 1902
to Colonel Shelton.*

138

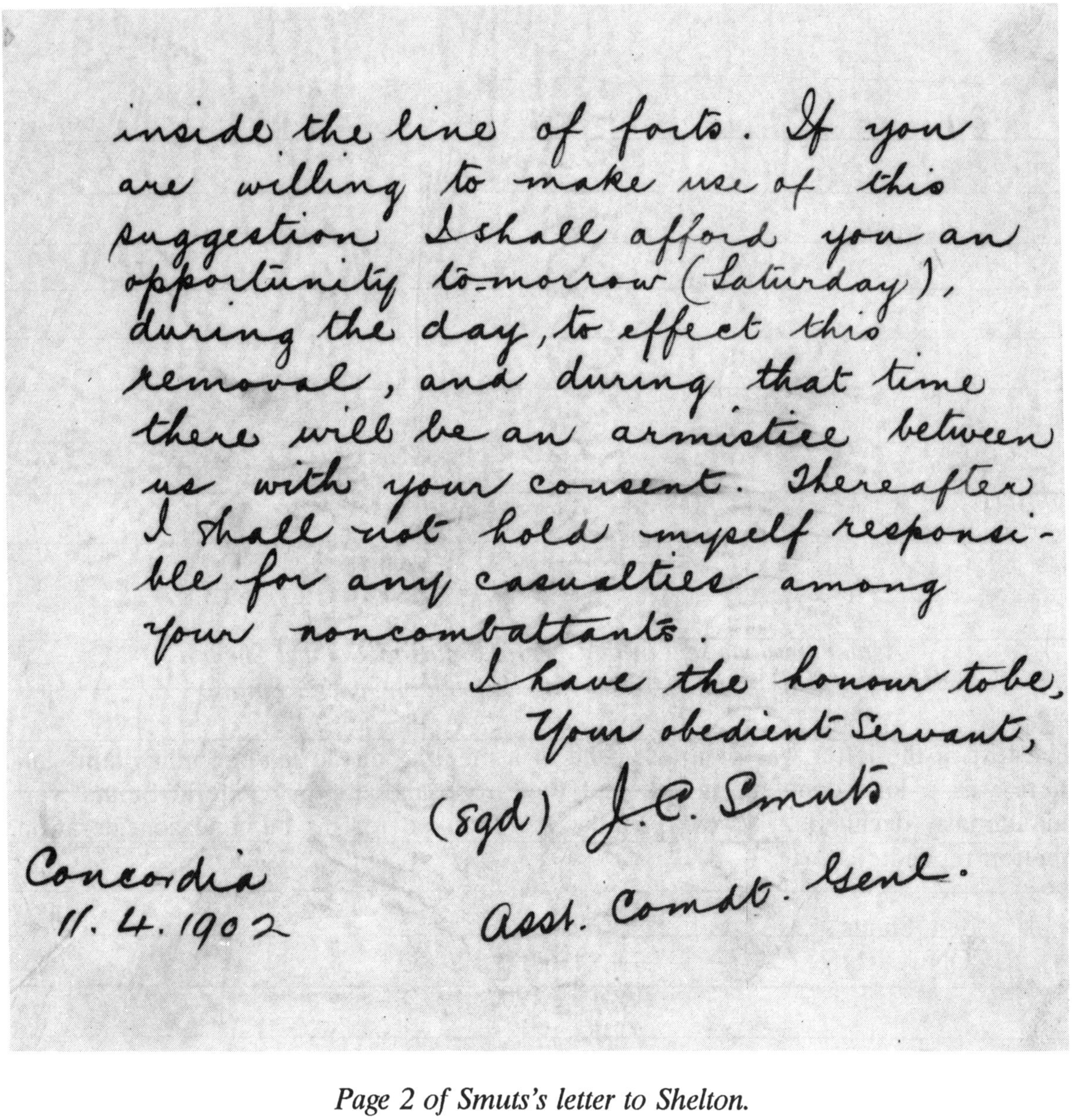

inside the line of forts. If you are willing to make use of this suggestion I shall afford you an opportunity to-morrow (Saturday), during the day, to effect this removal, and during that time there will be an armistice between us with your consent. Thereafter I shall not hold myself responsible for any casualties among your noncombattants.

I have the honour to be,
Your obedient Servant,
(sgd) J. C. Smuts
Asst. Comdt. Genl.

Concordia
11. 4. 1902

Page 2 of Smuts's letter to Shelton.

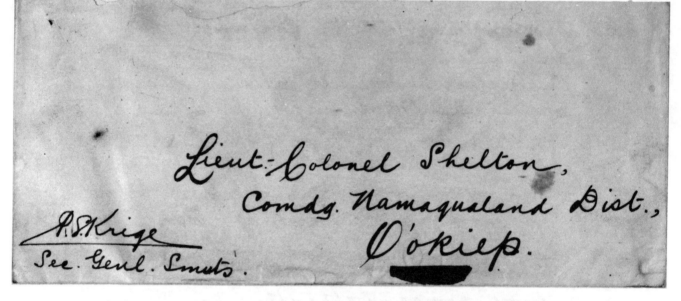

Actual envelope sent in by General Smuts to Colonel Shelton
signed on front by Tottie Krige, Secretary General Smuts.

The text of the letter was then discussed at a meeting of the leading inhabitants and there was a long debate. In the end the proposals sent by General Smuts were unanimously declined. However, Smuts was thanked for his humane consideration. Shelton replied:

"Gen. Smuts   District office
CONCORDIA   No. 3436 TB 17/18D
               April 11 1902
               O'OKiep
               NAMAQUALAND

"Sir:-

"(1) I have the honour to acknowledge the receipt of your letter of even date offering me an armistice tomorrow, and the opportunity to remove the non-combatants, women and children and ambulance hospitals from the town, to a locality outside the town in the direction of Springbok, but within the outerline of forts.

140

"I convened a meeting of the leading inhabitants of the town, and submitted your letter for their consideration, and decision, when one and all decided to remain where they are, and share the risks, as I have not means of affording the large number of women and children protection from the elements. I should have been inclined to favour your suggestion, but as it would be a case of camping on the veldt they prefer remaining where they are, and taking this chance. At the same time, I fully appreciate your humane consideration, and beg to thank you for the kindly offer you have made me.

"(2) While on the subject I wish to point out, on two occasions, Red Cross bearers have been fired upon while succouring wounded during the last few days. I feel sure you cannot approve of such action.

"(3) The gentlemen in charge of Mr Wrentmore's children declined to part with them unless he receives written instructions of Mr Wrentmore to do so.

"(4) I must apologize for again detaining your envoys so long a time, but the distance is considerable to the north gate & it took some time to get the committee together to lay your letter before them, I have been unable to forward the reply sooner.

"I have the honour to be Sir:-
your obedient Servant
signed W. Shelton
Lieut. Colonel
Commanding Namaqualand District."

After Colonel Shelton had read the text of the letter from Smuts, he sent a strongly worded message to Lieutenant Anstey at the north blockhouse which said:-

"From Col Shelton to Lt Anstey North Blockhouse 5.40pm 11.4.02. What have you done with the Boer envoys? I hold you responsible for their good treatment and comfort while they are with you. Letter from Gen Smuts received. I am calling a meeting of inhabitants and will lay before them Gen Smuts' proposals, after which will send reply to Gen Smuts's letter. Ask envoys to remain for reply."

The Commandant's reply to General Smuts was then given to the two envoys who began making their way back via the north gate of the outer defences. Shelton ensured the safe return of the two men to the Boer lines.

While the siege continued at Okiep the urgent messages which Shelton had sent earlier to Cape Town, via the sea from Port Nolloth were having results unknown to Colonel Shelton and his garrison. The British Military Authorities had despatched a substantial relief force which was commanded by Colonel H. Cooper, CMG, ADC. He was commanding the Cape Town District and had been appointed to lead the expedition and

Colonel Shelton's communication to Lt. Anstey regarding Boer Envoys.

Chart of entrance to Port Nolloth showing hazardous approach
Reproduced from an Admiralty Chart with permission of H.M.S.O.

the Namaqualand Field Force for the relief of Okiep and the immediate mining area. Meanwhile, Shelton had issued a report to all his officers and senior NCO's which was entitled 'Observations on the night attack made by the enemy on the inner blockhouses on the night of Thursday, the 10th day of April 1902'.

> "The enemy last night used 'Dynamite' with the object of blowing up the Blockhouses, but failed. He used bombs at 'SPRINGBOK' and succeeded in lodging one on top of a blockhouse and that Blockhouse surrendered. I have no doubt that had I been in a similar position I should have done the same. The garrison of 'SPRINGBOK' behaved splendidly, and held the place for 17 hours, and I do not consider the surrender any disgrace, while I deplore the loss of life, particularly the death of that gallant man Mr. Stewart MC.

143

*Troops of the Duke of Edinburgh's Own Volunteers
sighting Boer Commando near Klipfontein.*

Boer troops, using Martini Henri rifles, covering the railway line.

No. 3

General Smuts,

      CONCORDIA.

           Referring to my No 3464, para 2 of 11th inst.
I have the honour to bring to your notice a further case
of violation of the Geneva Convention under the folowing
circumstances.

           Hospital Orderly Frankenberg, Cape Garrison
Artillery, was sent out with two (2) stretcher bearers
carrying stretcher to bring in a wounded man from the
Range Kloof Blockhouse under the Red Cross Flag. The
bearer party was deliberately fired on several times un-
-til Pte Frankenberg was wounded in the chest and the
stretcher party had to return without the wounded man.

           This is the third instance of the Red Cross
Flag being fired on since operations commenced; and I
beg to enter the strongest protest against this appar-
-ently wilful, and gross violation of the Convention.

      I have the honour to be,

        Sir,

        Your obedient servant,

             Lieut-Colonel,

      Commanding Imperial Forces, O'OKIEP.

O'okiep,

   Namaqualand.

      12th April, 1902.

Letter from Colonel Shelton to Smuts re violation of the Geneva Convention

145

"As regards Concordia, we have to thank the Deputy Commandant for the Dynamite exploded on us last night. The Superintendent of the Namaqualand Copper Company, assured me that the Dynamite was hidden in such a way that it would be impossible for the enemy to find it. Whereas I have sworn evidence by persons present that he showed the enemy the place it was stored in. His action, it will be my duty to report to the proper quarter after this crisis is over.

"To come to last nights operations, the enemy attacked the 'Crow's Nest' after some six or seven hours sniping during the day. Under cover of heavy fire, enemy repeated their Springbok tactics with Dynamite bombs. Under this appalling bombardment, this small garrison surrendered and came out one by one. I believe the enemy passed through the lines apparently unnoticed by outer line of blockhouses in the extreme darkness. After the surrender of the Crow's Nest there was a lull in the fire for sometime.

"With regard to the terrific explosion last night, an expert, Mr. Henwood assures me that in his opinion, at least 25 to 30 lbs of dynamite was used. Major Edwards, Commanding Outer Lines well supported by Captain MacDonald SO at Fort Shelton held his own gallantly. The enemy got below the 'Fort' and cut the tanglefoot wire but Major Edwards' fire was so hot that they had had enough and returned and we had a little rest.

"We had a talk about 'Dynamite' this morning and at a general meeting, I asked an opinion whether we should send a protest to General Smuts or not. The opinion was that we had better not have anything to say to him and under the circumstances, I have decided to play the enemy with his own weapons and I intend to send up 12 bombs to 'Fort Shelton' which are to be used, and which I have named 'Major Edwards' Pills'.

"I urge you to impress on your men that the effect of the 'Dynamite' bark is much worse than its bite, and I am convinced if you keep up a heavy sustained fire, the enemy cannot get close enough to throw a bomb, and it cannot do you any harm. The enemy's object is to establish 'funk' with the coloured men, but you must reassure your men and inspire them with confidence.

"The behaviour of the garrison of Fort Shelton should be a splendid example to the rest of the garrison. The fine discipline leaves nothing to be desired, and if you insist on your men holding their ammunition until the enemy gets within short range, I feel confident we will hold O'OKiep, and keep the 'Flag flying' until relief reaches us. I noticed men lighting matches in the Defence Positions last night, officers should put an end to this, and should severely punish any man who does it, as it gives our position away.

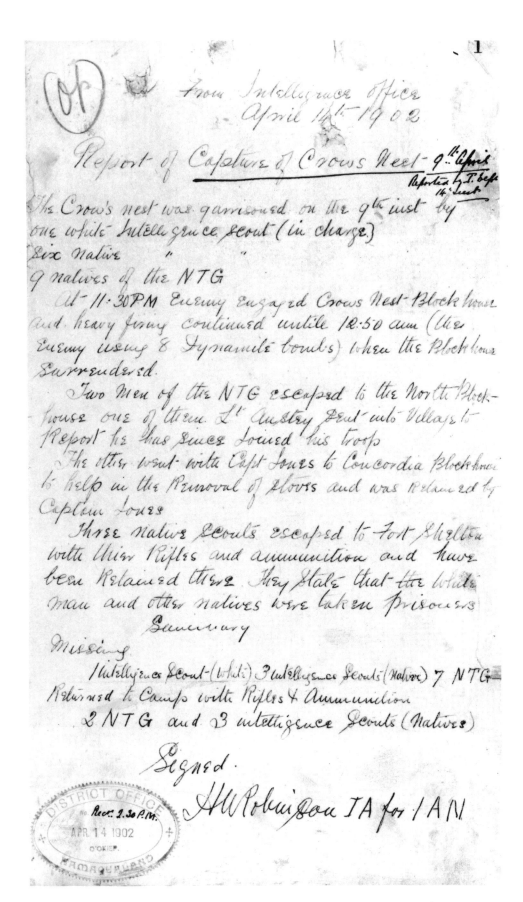

From Intelligence Office
April 14th 1902

Report of Capture of Crows Nest - 9th April
Reported by T. bept
14 Lieut

The Crow's nest was garrisoned on the 9th inst by
one white Intelligence scout (in charge.)
Six Native   "   "
9 natives of the NTG
   At 11·30PM Enemy engaged Crows Nest Block house
and heavy firing continued untile 12·50 am (the
Enemy using 8 Dynamite bombs) when the Block house
Surrendered.
   Two Men of the NTG escaped to the North Block-
house one of them Lt Anstey sent into Villays to
Report he has since Joined his troop
   The other went with Capt Jones to Concordia Block house
to help in the Removal of stores and was Retained by
Captain Jones
   Three Native Scouts escaped to Fort Shelton
with their Rifles and ammunition and have
been Retained there They state that the white
man and other natives were taken prisoners
                Summary
Missing
   1 Intelligence Scout (white) 3 Intelligence Scouts (Native) 7 NTG
Returned to Camp with Rifles & Ammunition
   2 NTG and 3 intelligence Scouts (Natives)

         Signed.
              HW Robinson IA for IAN

Intelligence report to Shelton from Robinson regarding the capture
of the Crow's Nest by Boers on 9th April, 1902

147

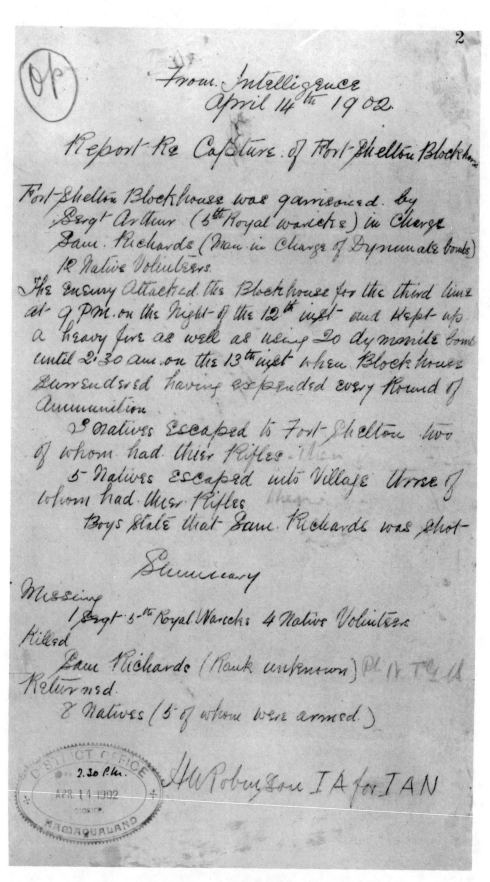

From Intelligence
April 14th 1902.

Report Re Capture of Fort Shelton Blockhouse

Fort Shelton Blockhouse was garrisoned by
Sergt Arthur (5th Royal Warwicks) in Charge
Sam Richards (Man in Charge of Dynamite bombs)
12 Native Volunteers.

The enemy attacked the Blockhouse for the third time
at 9 P.M. on the night of the 12th inst and kept up
a heavy fire as well as using 20 dynamite bombs
until 2.30 am on the 13th inst when Block house
Surrendered having expended every Round of
Ammunition

2 natives escaped to Fort Shelton two
of whom had their Rifles

5 Natives escaped into Village three of
whom had their Rifles

Boys state that Sam Richards was shot

Summary
Missing
1 Sergt 5th Royal Warcks 4 Native Volunteers
Killed
Sam Richards (Rank unknown)
Returned
8 Natives (5 of whom were armed)

HW Robinson IA for IAN

*A further intelligence report on the capture of the Fort Shelton Blockhouse
on 13th April, 1902*

"Another thing I noticed, many of the men lying with their 'Bandoliers' alongside them. This should be at once checked as natives waking from their sleep are naturally stupid and confused and would be liable to jump up and leave their 'bandoliers' behind them. It is dangerous practise and must be put a stop to.

"If you instill confidence in your men, in time they will get used to this sniping and take no notice of it. The enemy is in very great force and I read the names of the different commandos under General Smuts at the meeting today. Two commandos are 100 strong, remainder strength unknown. I have just received further information that Maritz was at Rietfontein a few days ago with 400 men. However, this number does not tally with the intelligence we have received and it is evidently native exaggeration. Colonel White reports two commandos under Pypers and Rudolph were advancing by Komaggas, so we are between two hot fires.

"We have two commandos from SW and those here now, and we have Maritz at Rietfontein with 400 men, and Mr. John Roux has sent in, himself, to state that Maritz said he intends to have O'OKiep.

"Officers should impress on the NCO's and men whom they may send as orderlies, messengers, etc. that they must not come to Head Quarter Office by the front entrance. There is an entrance from the back, which can be approached from the C.C. Coy's store under cover. Entry by the front is likely to attract attention from enemy to the Head Quarter Office, and I might as well fly a Flag indicating my whereabouts.

"When orderlies and messengers are sent to or from any blockhouse or Fort Shelton, they should invariably be unarmed.

"Officers are warned that the enemy approach the blockhouse disguised as goats in order to throw dynamite bombs, and every precaution should be taken to keep these animals at a distance.

"It would be well for Officers to impress on the men that every goat seen approaching a blockhouse represents a Boer and should be saluted with appropriate honours. Signed W. Shelton 11th April, 1902."

News had already filtered through to Okiep that a small force of Blue Jackets had landed from *HMS Forte* and *HMS Barracouta* at Port Nolloth. These sailors had made their way inland to the Waterworks at Jules Hoogte- which supplied the Port with drinking water. The main part of the relief force was now arriving at anchor off the Port. The approach to harbour was particularly treacherous and large vessels such as the Naval ships and transports had to disembark their cargoes into smaller boats which then were able to proceed to the inner harbour.

(Amended Scale)

Reduced under B. from the 14th Apl. 1902

SIEGE OF O'OKIEP

Scale of Rations

Framed by the Food Supply Committee,

April 6th, 1902.

Scale A. (EUROPEANS).

	MEAT.	BREAD.	SUGAR.	COFFEE.	TEA.	ONIONS.	POTATOES.	Salt
	lbs.	lbs.	ozs.	ozs.	ozs	lbs.	lbs.	
1. Adults male.	1	1	2	1/2	1/4	1/4	1/2	*1 lb packet per mth for each family.*
2. do. female.	1/2	1/2	1	1/4	1/8	1/8	1/4	
3. Children.	1/4	1/4	1/2	1/8	1/16	1/16	1/8	

Scale B. (COLOURED COMMUNITY)

		per week	*per week*	*per week*		Salt
1. Adults, male.	1/2	3/4	1/2 oz	2 oz	1/2 oz	*1 lb packet per week for each family.*
2. do. female.	1/4	1/4	1/2 oz	oz	1/2 oz	
3. Children.	1/8	1/4	1/2	1/8	1/16	

Scale C. (NATIVES).

		Mealies or Mealie meal			salt.
1. Adults	2ozs	1	1 5/7	3/7	3/7
2. Children.	2ozs	1/2	1 5/8	3/7	3/7

(signed) J. B. van Renen, C.C. and R.M.

Secretary.

O'okiep,

Namaqualand,

12th April, 1902.

Approved

W. Shelton

Lieut.-Colonel,
Commands Namaqualand District.

*Scale of Rations - approved by Col. Shelton on 14th April, 1902,
for the O'OKiep Garrison.*

150

HMS Sicilia had brought up from Cape Town five companies of the 4th East Surrey Regiment (Militia) under the command of Lieutenant Colonel Sullivan. The only soldiers who had seen any previous active service were the Colonel and one Captain.

With Colonel Cooper were Captain Parker, 5th Lancers, staff officer NFF, and two other officers of the Duke of Edinburgh's Own Volunteers who arrived at the Port on the afternoon of the 12th April 1902. While *HMS Forte* and *Barracouta* waited in the bay, Colonel Cooper was receiving intelligence reports on the actual locations of the Boer troops who had now advanced along the railway line from Anenous and had selected various strategic positions from which to oppose the relief column. The first reports Colonel Cooper read varied in accuracy. They indicated the Boers were within 5 miles of the Port, while others said the enemy was some 30 miles off and were destroying the railway and wooden viaducts near Anenous. In actual fact the Boers had only blown up a small culvert and certain parts of the railway line. General Van Deventer's main position being just west of Anenous. Their scouts were watching the formation of the relief force.

The main force of British troops now began to disembark from the larger ships and this was made more difficult by a heavy swell, while the horses and mules were being lowered into the boats by slings. Eventually the task was completed without the loss of life, men or animals, and the only item lost was a rifle.

Once ashore the troops advanced to the blockhouses guarding the approaches to the Port. By now night had fallen and the men had taken up their positions without blankets or rations, but Colonel Cooper had the situation well in hand and promised to send supplies up as soon as possible. He was concerned at the intelligence reports indicating that the Boers were advancing, although when he sent some scouts beyond Jules Hoogte in the railway line, to seek out the enemy, they found no trace of activity within the Sand Veld area because the Boers were positioned in the hills some distance further towards the higher ground, where they waited for the British relief column to approach. Back in Port Nolloth, Colonel Cooper had arranged for the 4th East Surrey men and the Duke of Edinburgh's Own Volunteers to be transported by the Cape Copper Company's train as far as the line would take them, the object being to discover what damage the Boers had done to the railway line.

At 8.30pm the train reached Jules Hoogte where two blockhouses were situated. These were manned by local black volunteers who were under the command of Captain MacDonald of the Namaqualand Border Scouts. Further along the railway line, at Anenous, there were two small blockhouses guarding the approach to the vitally important wooden viaducts. The garrisons were under the command of Lieutenants Meyrick and Moffat. Lieutenant Moffat was the Traffic manager for the Cape Company's railway and like Lieutenant Meyrick, he had refused to surrender to General Van Deventer's men when called upon to do so. Although heavily out-numbered they stubbornly refused to submit, and by their actions the important viaducts and that part of the railway line were saved from certain destruction.

The 4th East Surreys had now boarded a train, normally used for the transportation of Copper ore and went up the line. Following them in a second train were the Duke of

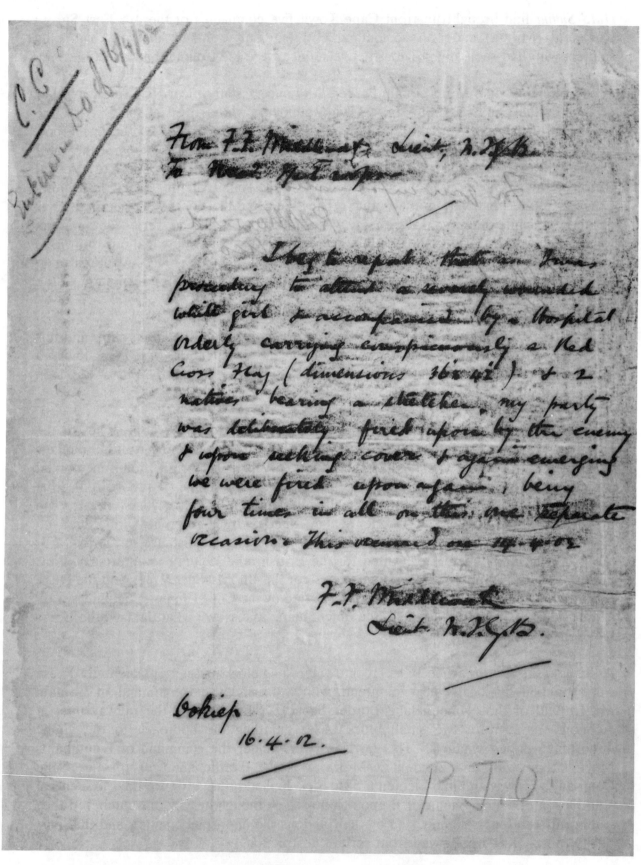

Report of firing on Red Cross Flag and stretcher bearers by the Boers when
attending severely wounded white girl - 14th April 1902.

Edinburgh's Own Volunteers with some platelayers who were to repair the 150 yards of track which had been totally destroyed by the Boer commando. The volunteers recruited from the Cape Town area were of mixed origin, Swedes, Germans and coloured and they formed one of the best fighting forces in the Colony. The two trains proceeded slowly because they were forced to stop every now and again so that the broken lines could be repaired.

Some 42 miles further along the track where it began to climb into more rocky and rugged terrain, the Boers had blown up a culvert and this was to take quite some time to reconstruct. Colonel Sullivan, who was supporting Colonel Cooper, ordered the troops to leave the trains and 'stand to arms' owing to the immediate danger of attack.

It was now only a short distance to Anenous, but it was so dark that it was difficult to maintain a guard on the plate layers, who were working as fast as possible. The second train was now sent back to Port Nolloth to pick up more troops to reinforce the advancing column. Colonel Cooper had also brought up some artillery which was commanded by Lieutenant Ironside who was shortly to distinguish himself in this campaign; and later in the Great World War of 1914-1918 which was to follow. He became the well known General 'Tiny' Ironside, a great soldier and linguist. Ironside's Field Guns were fifteen pounders of 44 Battery, Royal Field Artillery and formed an essential part of the main relief column which was soon to be involved in action.

As the relief column began to concentrate, the moon appeared from behind the clouds, revealing the mountainous country which lay ahead. A short distance away the outline of a very large mountain became visible. This was Klipfontein rising to over 3,400 feet. Colonel Cooper decided to occupy the summit, because he realized from intelligence reports and maps that it was vitally important to command this highest point. The column moved off silently into the sandy desert which eventually gave way to the rocky foothills of the mountain. Anenous was the main objective now. If Cooper's column could reach that point his troops would be well on their way to Okiep and the besieged garrison. General Van Deventer's forces were watching their progress in the moonlight, but their leader decided not to attack the British troops just yet.

Back in Okiep the siege continued with increasing hostility on both sides. It was now the twelfth day of the siege and though the garrison was putting up a good defence, the Boers were beginning to press home their attacks from both sides of the hills. At this stage of the siege the commandos were confident of taking Okiep.

General Jan Smuts now decided to capture the place and secure the valuable copper mines and all property. At 10am the Boers attacked with great determination. Again the exchange of fire was fierce but with little effect. The main Boer objectives were the Shelton blockhouse and Fort Shelton. These two Forts had been singled out for complete destruction by Smuts and his men because when they were put out of action the way would be open for the Boers to advance into the town - or so they thought. The attacking Boers had now occupied some ridges laying between the two blockhouses north of the approaches to Okiep but as the night was dark, it was difficult for the defending garrison to determine exactly where the enemy's fire was coming from. The Boers were determined to deliver a decisive blow to the outer defence system and capture it. In reply, the Okiep northern positions maintained sustained fire all along their line until the Boers were silenced in some areas, except in the vicinity of Shelton blockhouse. Here the attackers threw a large number of dynamite grenades with considerable effect. After a desperate and stubborn resistance the Shelton blockhouse fell. General Maritz, who took part in the attack threw a 20 pound dynamite bomb onto the roof of the Shelton blockhouse blowing it in, and he had to stand on another man's shoulder to do it. This bomb forced the garrison, which had expended all their ammunition, to surrender. Maritz's bravery should have warranted a gallantry award.

The north blockhouse was also subjected to heavy bombing and rifle fire, although, under the command of Lieutenant Anstey, it held out bravely. The noise was tremendous and echoed throughout the area like thunder. "The behaviour of the garrison of this blockhouse reflected the greatest credit on Lieut Anstey and his men", wrote Colonel Shelton later. At 1.15am the Boer fire on the blockhouses was completely silenced with the remainder of the night passing in relative peace. The Boers reported their success against the Shelton blockhouse to General Smuts who was pleased to hear of their progress. As the telegraph wire had been cut during the attack on the north blockhouse, it was essential to repair this line. Sergeant Peart RE bravely carried out this work under fire from snipers while the garrison did its best to provide covering fire. He managed to restore the line. The casualties of Okiep troops during attacks on the Shelton blockhouse were two killed and five wounded. Sixteen dead bodies of Boer troops were found near the scene of the action.

The commando had undoubtedly suffered severely. A total of 6,398 rounds of ammunition was used by the garrison during these operations. While Okiep enjoyed a little peace later that morning the defending troops were already bracing themselves for further dynamite grenade attacks, but it was now the turn of Okiep's big gun - the nine pounder. Captain Freeland had been observing where the Boer fire had been coming from during the battle because many of the Boer riflemen were armed with Martini Henry Rifles which did not have smokeless ammunition and so revealed their positions. He opened fire on these positions and soon silenced the sniping.

During this exchange of fire there was, unfortunately, a gross violation of the Geneva Convention by the Boers, and Colonel Shelton felt compelled to write a strong protest to General Smuts.

> "April 12 1902 Namaqualand
> General Smuts,
> CONCORDIA.
>
> "Referring to my No 3464 para 2 of 11th last. I have the honour to bring to your notice a further case of violation of the Geneva Convention under the following circumstances.
>
> "Hospital Orderly Frankenberg, Cape Garrison Artillery, was sent out with two (2) stretcher bearers carrying stretcher to bring in a wounded man from the Range Kloof blockhouse under the Red Cross Flag. The bearer

party was deliberately fired on several times until Pte Frankenberg was wounded in the chest and the stretcher party had to return without the wounded man.

"This is the third instance of the Red Cross Flag being fired on since operations commenced; and I beg to enter the strongest protest against this apparently wilful, and gross violation of the Convention.

"I have the honour to be
Sir,
Your obedient servant,

signed W. Shelton
Lieut-Colonel
Commanding Imperial Forces, O'OKiep

"O'OKiep
Namaqualand
12th April 1902"

Colonel Shelton had pointed out a previous contravention of the Geneva Agreement in his letter to Smuts on 11th April.

The current state of affairs at Okiep was reported to the headquarters in Cape Town by a special runner sent to Port Nolloth with urgent despatches. He went through the Boer lines in darkness at 11.30pm on the 11th April and was successful in reaching the Port unharmed a few days later. Shelton's urgent news was immediately sent by the Gunboat to Hondeklip Bay where it was telegraphed to HQ in Cape Town. Here General Settle in turn sent it to General French.

Port Nolloth had now been strongly fortified by the landing of more guns from *HMS Barracouta*. These weapons included Maxim machine guns and Nordenfeldt quick-firing guns, and these new weapons now greatly increased the defensive power of the garrison.

In Okiep, in order to exercise a certain amount of control over the opening of fire, Shelton had instituted a system of hooter signals which he notified to all officers commanding sections of the inner line of defence:
No. 1 position (Captain Burke) a single blast of hooter - duration 2 seconds.
No. 2 position (Captain Crozier) 2 blasts - with interval of 2 seconds.
No. 3 position (Captain Townsend) 3 blasts.
No. 4 position (Captain Thompson) 4 blasts.
The general 'Cease Fire' for all in the line will be a sustained blast of hooter lasting 30 seconds.

While Okiep remained in a state of siege, 45 miles away to the north-west, Colonel Cooper's relief column had now advanced along the railway line to Anenous without a single shot being fired. The two wooden viaducts were now visible just ahead of them

POST OFFICE TELEGRAPHS.

G.P.O. 808.
T. 30.

A.

Prefix	Code	Class
Office of Origin and Service Instructions.	Words.	Sent.
	Charge.	At ____ M
		To
		By

No. of Message

Office Stamp.

Stamps to be affixed here and
Obliterated by clear impressions of
Office Date Stamp.

A Receipt for the Charges on this Telegram may
be obtained, price Twopence.

FROM

O.C.

Please Write Distinctly.

TO

Lieut Anstey
Nott B.H.

The Signal of the approach of
Col. Cooper's Relief Column will
be six rockets sent up at
intervals of ten seconds each.

By order
Alan Borcherds
Capt S.O.

8.15 p.m.
Nott B.H.

Repeated to all outer Defences

Signature of Sender
AB

Address _____

N.B.—The Department is not liable for losses incurred through
incorrect transmission, delay or non-delivery of Telegrams

*A message from the Commanding Officer to Lt. Anstey at the North Blockhouse
indicating the signa procedure for the approach of Colonel Cooper's column.*

156

as the line ran through the rugged countryside towards the highest point - Klipfontein Mountain.

Colonel Cooper ordered his troops to get what rest they could while one company remained on guard.

General Van Deventer's men, who had been watching Cooper's advance, began withdrawing to a higher position towards the summit of Klipfontein where they waited for the British to begin climbing the steep mountain. Colonel Cooper having arrived at Anenous on the morning of 14th April, bringing with him the remaining companies of the East Surrey Regiment from Port Nolloth, sent one company with a Maxim machine gun about half a mile beyond Anenous to guard the village from the east and south. The other company was ordered 3 miles up the line to guard the wooden viaducts against any further attempts to destroy them. Cooper's two companies began building sangars (circular, bullet-proof, dry-stone wall enclosures to protect troops unable to dig into rocky ground) and small defensive positions while awaiting further reinforcements. These came a few days later. The Duke of Edinburgh's Own Volunteers arrived and also advanced further along the Cape Copper Company's railway towards the viaducts. Colonel Cooper was now concentrating his force, knowing the Boers were waiting for them at Klipfontein. This town was a further 8 miles along the line and was in difficult country. In and around Okiep, the battle still continued.

At 10am on Sunday, 13th April, the Boers launched a fierce attack from the eastern ridges and the Crow's Nest, which they now occupied. This was immediately countered by the garrison's 'nine pounder' supported by fire from the outer defences. Three shells from the field gun exploded around the Crow's Nest and the enemy was forced to withdraw from this position. Fire from the hills on both sides of the town then increased and continued until dusk. It was a prelude to a new, determined, but unsuccessful attack by the Boers on the garrison's blockhouses which formed part of the formidable defences of the town.

The general situation on the 14th April was that General Smuts was maintaining the pressure on Okiep. Van Deventer was waiting for Colonel Cooper's relief column to advance up the western side of Klipfontein Mountain where he intended to engage it. Colonel White was still 'locked up' in Garies with little chance of breaking out. The only hope Okiep had was Colonel Cooper's determination to scatter the boer commando with his relief column and push Van Deventer's troops back from Klipfontein along the railway to Steinkopf and to drive them out of the mining area.

Okiep was holding out well, but at a cost. Casualties were still increasing.

CHAPTER 10

THE RELIEF COLUMN ADVANCES

General Van Deventer's main force was now well positioned among the rocks on the summit of the mountain at Klipfontein, eight miles east of Anenous, where they waited for Colonel Cooper's men. The relief column had paused to allow a squadron of the 5th Lancers, led by Captain Parker, to join them. This squadron formed part of a force of Cavalry which included the 118th Imperial Yeomanry, 40 men of the Cape Mounted Police and two 15 pounder field guns, under the command of Lieutenant Ironside. This brought Cooper's force to roughly 250 men.

Van Deventer's men had not been idle while Cooper was collecting his force. The Boers destroyed the railway line in many places, the area between Klipfontein and Steinkopf being the worst effected. Seeing the steady progress of the relief column the Boer scouts reported back to Van Deventer who decided to withdraw his men to the hills on the eastern side of the large mountain.

Cooper had now made his plans to force the Boers from the top of Klipfontein and down the other side towards Steinkopf and open country. If successful, he would be able to bring his field guns into action and dislodge the Boers from any positions opposing him.

15 pound field gun shelling Boers.
Colonel Cooper's Relief Column.

Lieutenant Ironside had already brought up his shrapnel shells and was calculating the fuse settings so that they would explode above the Boers where he had pinpointed his targets. From beyond the hills that lay ahead of the column loud explosions were heard as the Boers blew up more of the railway line and the mining property at Nababeep, using the large quantities of dynamite they had captured at Concordia. At this point Colonel Cooper despatched two runners to Colonel Shelton in Okiep to give him up to date information regarding the progress of the relief force. They arrived safely.

Van Deventer's scouts kept him well informed on the movements of the column which was now advancing in battle order. Cooper's men were searching for the 'unseen enemy' who were well concealed.

The Boer General summed up the situation and sent a report to General Smuts recommending withdrawal from his present positions in order to confront Cooper's relief column further down the line near Steinkopf. General Smuts agreed, and Van Deventer gave orders to his men to blow the main water tanks at Klipfontein - these explosions were heard by the advancing British troops. As the Boers withdrew from their positions the advancing British troops found evidence of their hasty departure. Strewn on the ground between the rocks and bushes were bits of paper, cigarette stubs, empty cans, loose cartridges and ashes from small fires.

When the advanced force of the relief column was about to reach the summit of the great mountain, it halted in order to wait for Colonel Cooper and the rest of the troops.

Meanwhile, over the high mountain in Okiep, Colonel Shelton and his men were anxiously waiting further news of Cooper's Column. Since the capture of the two outlying blockhouses by the Boers a few days earlier, there had been much more action against the stubborn little garrison. But the battle was not one-sided, intelligence reports from black agents brought news of the hospital at Concordia being full of Boer wounded. Medical supplies were now running low and this greatly added to the hardship of the Boers. General Smuts ordered a further situation report from Van Deventer. This was sent and Smuts decided that Cooper's force must be halted at Steinkopf which was a suitable location for this purpose.

The railway from Klipfontein entered a small valley about a mile long, and at the end of it the ground rose for several feet, forming a rocky ridge, and behind it the terrain dropped away rapidly to the plains below. Steinkopf lay close under this ridge which provided an excellent defensive position. Troops concealed there could cover the relatively narrow approach down the valley. The centre of this position was a natural fortress with its flanks protected by the hills.

Colonel Cooper's men entered Klipfontein only to find it a scene of desolation. Before withdrawing to Steinkopf the Boers had destroyed everything they possibly could. The massive water tank had been blown to bits. The houses had been looted and left in a filthy state and much of the furniture had been destroyed. Cooper immediately sent scouts forward towards Steinkopf and the surrounding district to reconnoitre the enemy positions. They soon located large parties of Boers and after a fierce exchange of rifle

From Col Cooper   To Col Shelton
Klipfontein   Ookiep
6 pm 22 April 1902
N.H. I have not received any news from
you since that brought in by Robinson
up to 19th inst. Have you been unable to
get news through?

I have established a signalling
station on Klipfontein mountain which
was answered by you this morning,
but I have not yet received any
intelligible message. The Klipfontein
signal station will be open daily from
9am to 12 noon and from 2 pm to 4.30 pm

I have not yet received any reply from
Genl Smuts to Genl Botha's telegram

From what I gather Maritz is commanding
against White and VandeVenter against me
under general command of Smuts.

Col. Callwell should be here today and
I hope shortly that his mounted troops
will make their presence felt. I hope

your wounded are doing well especially
the women.

White has been in communication
with Cape Town via Lamberts Bay as late
as the 73th inst.

I am sending you summaries of
general news which will be of interest
to you and the inhabitants of Ookiep.

Cooper   Colonel
Comdg. N.7.7.

DISTRICT OFFICE
No 8.30 am.
APR 24 1902
O'KIEP.
NAMAQUALAND

Replied to under O.K. 3. T.K. 27/5.

*On April 24th, 1902 Colonel Shelton received the above message from
Colonel Cooper by runner who arrived at 8.30am that morning*

fire returned to Klipfontein to report that Steinkopf was strongly held. He ordered Lieutenant Colonel Callwell, his second in command, to make a reconnaissance towards the enemy positions with as many mounted men as possible. They moved off the same afternoon (21st April) and were soon near the main Boer stronghold. The commando, having also posted their scouts and look-outs, saw Callwell approaching and waited for him to advance within the range of their rifles. When they opened fire, one of Callwell's troops was seriously wounded. The British force returned fire and attempted to attack the Boer position, but eventually after a hot encounter Callwell realised his numbers were too weak and ordered his men to retire. Lieutenant Mather and two other men were badly wounded. These casualties were taken back to Klipfontein and Lieutenant Colonel Callwell gave a full report of the fight to Cooper. In Okiep Colonel Shelton, realising the relief column was now at Klipfontein, sent a message to Lieutenant Anstey at the north blockhouse telling him that the signal of the approach of Colonel Cooper's relief column would be 6 rockets sent up at intervals of 10 seconds.

Now that Colonel Cooper had reached the summit of the Klipfontein Mountain he set up a Heliograph Signalling Station in order to contact the garrison in Okiep in the valley below. At the same time Lieutenant Ironside brought up his two fifteen pounders and began shelling the Boer positions at Steinkopf. One of the shrapnel shells exploding over the enemy positions, killed several Boer troops and many horses.

The tide was beginning to turn against the Boer forces of Van Deventer and Smuts. Nevertheless, the brave and experienced commandos had dug in and their General was determined not to yield Steinkopf without fierce resistance.

While Ironside's gunners continued firing, Cooper's heliograph was flashing messages to Shelton in Okiep and making contact for the first time since the relief expedition had landed. These heliograph messages were recorded by Sergeant Gerter, 5th Battalion Royal Warwicks, whose first indication of this contact with the relieving force was when he saw a winking light high up in the mountains to the north. It caused great jubilation in the garrison. Colonel Shelton sent word to everyone in the town and to his men in the outer defences, to remain calm and vigilant as the Boers would probably also have seen the heliograph. No sooner had the message from Shelton been circulated to all the garrison than the Boers opened heavy fire from the hills which was returned by the garrison.
The first heliograph message Sergeant Gerter took down at 12 noon on the 22nd April was:

> "From Colonel Cooper to Colonel Shelton, Good morning very glad to open communication good luck to you all. How are wounded getting on especially the women. I shall be in to-morrow at 4.30"

The Boers now realised Okiep was in signal contact with the relief column, and this made them all the more determined to fight on. The garrison look-outs had noticed the Boers digging in at the rear of the Shelton blockhouse where, at night, wagons arrived from the direction of Concordia, carrying supplies and ammunition. It was now intensely cold at night and the trenches provided a certain amount of protection from it. Shelton sent further messages to Generals French and Settle and the GOC Southern Command with a special report to the Intelligence Department at Cape Town. They were taken by men who had to infiltrate the enemy lines, and they were all extremely brave volunteers who knew exactly what would happen to them if they were caught by the Boers. Shelton was also able to send a message to Colonel White who was still bottled up in Garies. While the relief column advanced towards the besieged area, Colonel Cooper received a message from Shelton which had been sent to Anenous at 8pm on the 21st. This informed him of the state of the wounded and the general situation in Okiep as far as supplies and morale were concerned. There was now a great deal of stress on the garrison and civilian population, especially the women and children.

At 8pm on 22nd April a message was sent to Colonel Cooper to advise him that the garrison was about to make a sortie against the enemy. Shelton had ordered 25 men of the Namaqualand Border Scouts to be ready for mounted duty with their bandoliers full. The men assembled with their horses in the northern line and awaited orders. Scouts went out to reconnoitre the area of the Crow's Nest, and reported that many Boers entrenched. On this information at 10pm that night, QMS Cawker NBS took a patrol of twelve men from Fort Shelton to attack the unsuspecting Boers. At about 4.30am Cawker and his men attacked and took the Boers completely by surprise. After a sharp exchange of fire the Boers were driven out of the Crow's Nest and retreated in the direction of Concordia, their HQ, taking with them several wagons. Sergeant Cawker's men captured a Lee Enfield rifle which was marked South Wales Borderers and had three cartridges in the magazine, a full bandolier and six blankets. One of Cawker's men was slightly wounded, and the dead body of a Boer was left on the Concordia road. Cawker's troops withdrew to Fort Shelton and reported that the enemy had now occupied the eastern ridge with a force of about 100 men. This sortie had been a great success and on their return Sergeant Cawker and his men were congratulated by Colonel Shelton.

At about 8.30am the Boers again opened fire from the eastern ridges, killing one man and wounding two more at Fort Shelton, and at the same time firing from the western ridges caused a few casualties in the town. During these exchanges of fire, to which the Garrison was becoming accustomed, Cooper and Shelton were also exchanging Heliograph signals. The firing continued until 6.30pm and the attention of the firers was then diverted by a full eclipse of the moon. The number of casualties especially among the non-combatants in Okiep, was causing concern to Shelton. However, he had seen that the inhabitants were not keeping under cover and had a tendency to wander out into the open, thus presenting easy targets. He therefore ordered all non-combatants, especially the parents of children, to remain under cover unless they were carrying out official duties for the garrison.

A further heliograph message was received from Colonel Cooper at 10.50am on the 23rd April which said that he hoped to be in Okiep by the end of the month but this depended on the Boers. At 5.30pm on the 23rd April a patrol of about 30 Boers approached the Crow's Nest Kloof, moving along the Concordia road. When fired on from the north blockhouse, two saddles were emptied, the patrol withdrew, and there was no further activity that night.

162

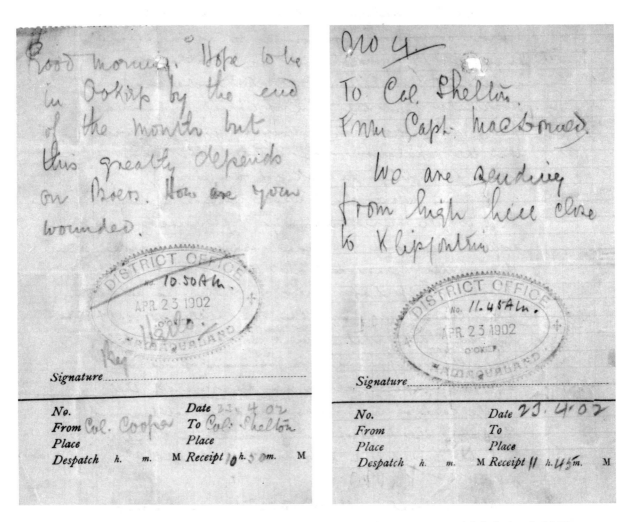

Two heliograph messages to Okiep received on the morning of 23rd April 1902.

Concordia, 38.
25. 4. 1902.

Lieut.- Colonel Shelton,
    Comdg. Namaqualand District,
        O'okiep.

Sir,

I wish to return to the subject about which I wrote to you on a previous occasion, when I suggested that you should remove the non-combatant population and the Ambulance Hospitals from the town of O'okiep to another place within your lines. Your reply to this was that the population had decided for themselves to undergo the risks of the siege.

In all deference, however, I should say that it fell more within your province, as an experienced and humane soldier, to decide this matter than to leave the decision to people who perhaps view my letter as an idle threat, and who have no real idea of the great danger they run. I wish to acquaint you with my opinion – the opinion of one who has had experience in similar cases – that in the case of the noncombatants not leaving the town the lives of many women and children will be sacrificed before the end of the siege.

The removal will of course be accompanied by difficulties, but may eventually prove to have been the wisest and most humane course.

I am prepared to agree to an armistice for today, tomorrow, and the day after (25-27th incl.)

Page 1 of last historic letter from General Smuts to Colonel Shelton dated 25th April 1902

164

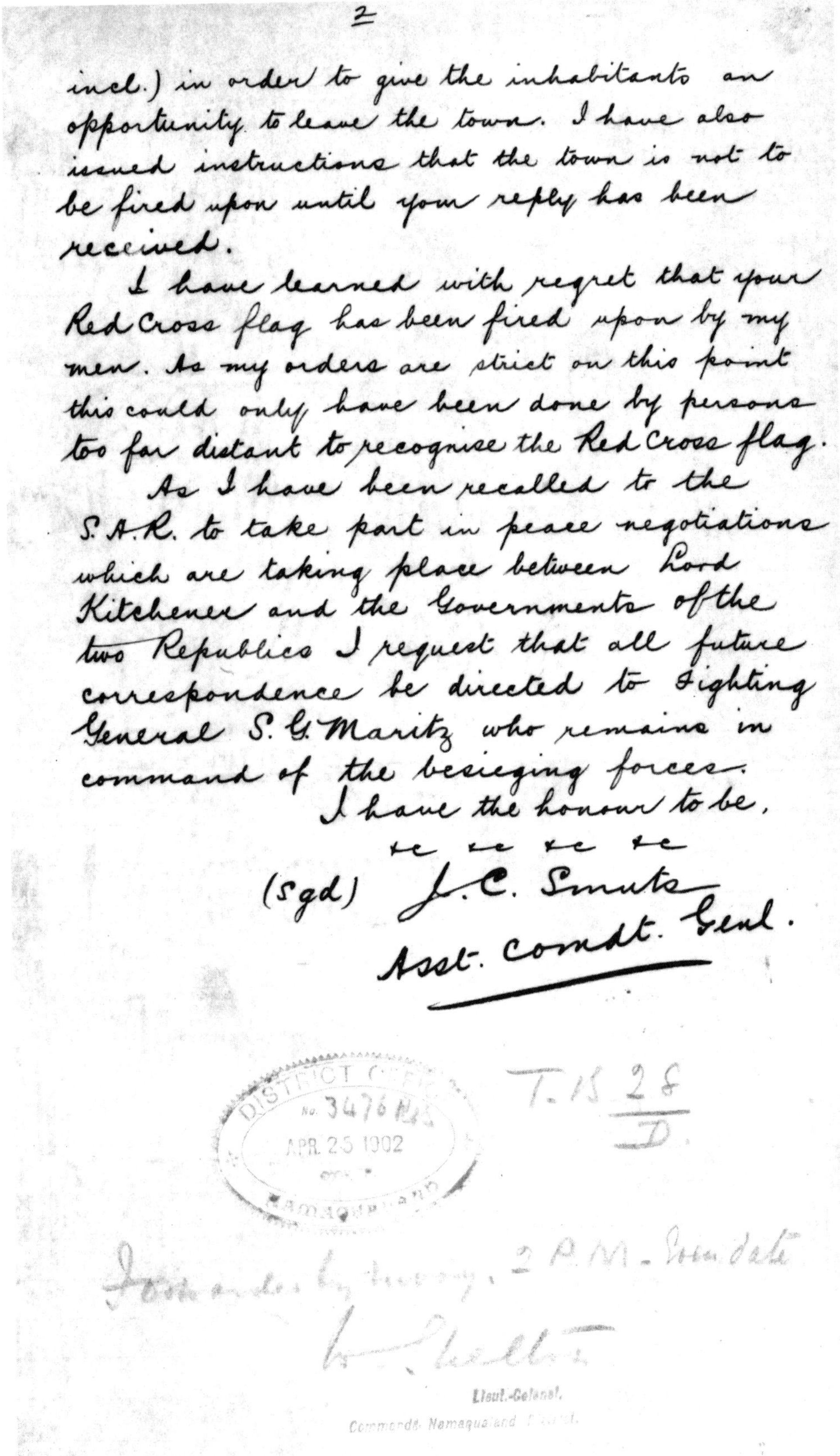

2

incl.) in order to give the inhabitants an opportunity to leave the town. I have also issued instructions that the town is not to be fired upon until your reply has been received.

I have learned with regret that your Red Cross flag has been fired upon by my men. As my orders are strict on this point this could only have been done by persons too far distant to recognise the Red Cross flag.

As I have been recalled to the S.A.R. to take part in peace negotiations which are taking place between Lord Kitchener and the Governments of the two Republics I request that all future correspondence be directed to Fighting General S. G. Maritz who remains in command of the besieging forces.

I have the honour to be,
&c &c &c &c
(Sgd) J. C. Smuts
Asst. Comdt. Genl.

DISTRICT [illegible]
No. 3476
APR. 25 1902
NAMAQUALAND

T.K. 28
D.

Forwarded by [illegible] 2 P.M. - same date
[illegible] Shelton
Lieut.-Colonel,
Commdg. Namaqualand [illegible]

Page 2 of letter from Smuts to Shelton

Reply No4

General Smuts,

    A. C. General,

        CONCORDIA.

Sir,

    I have the honour to acknowledge receipt of your letter of even date, renewing the offer you made me on the 11th inst, of an Armistice to enable me to remove Non-combatant population, and the Ambulance Hospitals from the Town of O'OKIEP to another place within my Lines.

    In thanking you for your courtesy, and further consideration, I may add that nothing has occurred since receipt of your previous letter on the subject, to in--cline me to alter the decision therein expressed.

    I note your remarks relative to the violation of Geneva Convention by your Troops. And also that you are leaving NAMAQUALAND for VEREENIGING, to take part in peace negoiations, and that General S. G. Maritz will act as your Locum-Tenens.

    I have the honour to be

        Sir,

        Your Obedient Servant,

            (signed) W. Shelton, Lieut:Colonel,
                Commanding Namaqualand District.

Colonel Shelton's reply to letter of General Smuts of 25th April 1902

At 8.30am on the 25th April, a Boer messenger, under the 'White Flag of Truce' brought another letter from General Smuts to Colonel Shelton. Shelton read the letter and considered the offer of the 'armistice' and evacuation of the non-combatants. For the time being firing on the town had ceased as Smuts had promised, but Shelton could foresee much difficulty in transporting women, children, the older men and any wounded to the open veld where they would have no protection. Again he decided to call a meeting of the leading inhabitants to place before them the offer made by Smuts. The envoy was told to wait while the talks took place and after hearing all the opinions on the matter it was unanimously decided to decline General Smuts' proposal, as had been the case in the 11th April. Due note was taken of Smuts' regret that the Garrison's Red Cross Flag and stretcher bearers had been fired upon. It was also noted that General Smuts had said he was about to leave the area and take part in peace negotiations, but his statement that 'Fighting General S.G.Maritz' was to take over command of the besieging forces was not good news for Okiep for it meant the Boers will continue to besiege and attack the town. This letter was the last of the personal exchanges between Smuts and Shelton, and the armistice expired that evening, on the return of Smuts' messenger with Shelton's reply.

Heavy cloud over the area prevented any signalling by heliograph, so messages had to be carried by runners - a most dangerous task through territory held by the Boers.

167

CHAPTER 11

GENERAL SMUTS LEAVES FOR PEACE TALKS

Meanwhile Colonel Cooper's column, still concentrating more men in order to drive the Boers from their stronghold at Steinkopf, was still four miles from Okiep. Cooper, preparing for an all-out assault on Van Deventer called his Artillery and Cavalry officers to a council of war to decide on the best plan of attack Steinkopf was not going to be easy to take.

The obvious solution to the problem was to surround the Boer position but this was not possible for two reasons. First the extremely difficult terrain on its flanks and secondly the risk of the unacceptable number of casualties the Boers could inflict on troops trying to outflank them. And so the only course left open to him was a frontal attack by infantry, supported by cavalry, and preceded by a heavy artillery barrage. This barrage, under Lieutenant Ironside's direction, caused many casualties in the Boer position, and the sound of it could be clearly heard in Okiep, but the Boers stayed put, and fought back with accurate rifle fire, paying no regard to the casualties that Ironside was inflicting. After a while there was a lull in the battle, enabling both sides to take stock of the situation and attend to the wounded.

Lieutenant Ironside's Field Guns had been accurate enough to dislodge some of the Boers from their concealed positions, but their main force was still determined that Cooper's troops would not capture Steinkopf. Colonel Cooper decided to wait until he could bring up substantial reinforcements now assembled at Anenous, and he sent orders for them to move up as quickly as possible to the combat zone. While this was going on Lieutenant Ironside's Field Guns continued to shell Steinkopf and the surrounding area.

The net was now closing in on the commando forces, fighting against increasing odds. When General Smuts prepared to leave his troops and travel through the British lines to Port Nolloth, he realised the negotiations he was to attend at Vereeniging had serious implications for the Afrikaner people. He spoke to all his troops before leaving for the Port, telling them the war was not over and they must be resolute in their cause. He bade Van Deventer and the men farewell as he left, taking his safe conduct pass to allow him through the British lines.

On the 26th April General Smuts, accompanied by 'Tottie' Krige, his military secretary, and Deneys Reitz, set off under a flag of truce towards the British troops. He was escorted by commandos who were uneasy about his safety. Colonel Cooper and Lieutenant Colonel Callwell RFA, his second in command, came out to meet the party and greeted General Smuts and his colleagues. Smuts remained quiet and made little or no comment as the rode through the British lines. After a short distance General Smuts, Krige and Reitz dismounted and their horses were taken by the escort. After singing the commando's hymn, Smuts' men turned their horses in the direction of their own troops and galloped off with a great cheer for their leader whom they had served so well.

Heliograph message from Colonel Cooper to Lt. Col Shelton regarding General Smuts' route to peace talks plus coded message regarding Cooper's advance and Boer troop movements

TEXT OF MESSAGE: NK. General Smuts is expected at Klipfontein at 9 am on 26th inst. en route to Cape Town to join Boer delegation at Vereeniging. The numbers in my front are apparently few and I shall attempt to reach Steinkopf on the afternoon of 26th. Let me know as soon as possible the latest estimate of numbers and whereabouts of enemy at Concordia, Ratelpoort and Nababeep.

B. POST OFFICE TELEGRAPHS.

Prefix *XB* Code *63* A** Class _____ No. of Message } *1*

		Office of Origin and Service Instructions.	Words.		Office Stamp.
Received {	At *11.25* A.M. From *KL* By *Genter*	*KL*	*84*	Sent { At *11.29* A.M. To *ABB* By *Nelson*	*76*

From	To
Col Cooper	Col ~~Cooper~~ Shelton

No. 11.40 a.m. APR 26 1902

Your	Helio	Message		25th
has	been	received		shall
be	glad	of	three	white
identi-	many	thanks	for	information
about	forage	am	moving	my
headquarters	from	Amenous	to	
Klipfontein	today	Glad	you	declined
Armistice	meaning	is	beginning	to
feel	pressure	from	this	side
also	from	South		hope
to	occupy	Maaisfontein	tonight	Your
OK 3	has	not	yet	been
received	Have	you	got	Major
Scott – Moor ASC	with	you		

Heliograph message from Colonel Cooper regarding his advance to Klipfontein

W.A.R. & Sons.—C2*96.6.000,000.10.1900.

B. POST OFFICE TELEGRAPHS.

Prefix X B Code ____ Class ____

No. of Message } 2

Received	At 9 A.M.	Office of Origin and Service Instructions.	Words.	Sent	At A.M.	Office Stamp.
From KL	Delayed through fog NN		To Add	28th		
By Steller			Mess			

From

Col Cooper

Klipfontein

No. 9.30 A.M. ... Shelton
APR 28 1902
O'OKIEP. O'Kiep,

DISTRICT OFFICE
NAMAQUALAND

	NN.	April	27th	
Sorry	fog	interferes	with	signals
yesterday.	Had	a	try	to
get	into	STEINKOPF	on	Friday
but	hope	to	get	in
there	to-day.	Probably	my	advance
made	enemy	more	alert	round
you.	Be	very	careful	Boers
dont	rush	you.	Keep	me
well	informed	of	all	news.
about	enemy.	You	have	never
yet	told	me	who.	was
responsible	for	surrender	of	CONCORDIA.
Please	do,	so	as	inquiry
must	be	held.	Funds	came
in	yesterday			

W.A.B. & Sons.—CH/96.5,000,000.10,1900.

Heliograph message confirming Cooper's attempt to take Steinkopf and requesting information regarding the surrender of Concordia

The British had arranged a guard of honour to meet General Smuts at the railway line which was called to attention when the General came to board the train to Port Nolloth. In order to keep Colonel Shelton informed of what was happening, Colonel Cooper had been sending heliograph messages to him, and confirmed them by sending runners with written messages.

The weather had deteriorated and more heavy clouds brought torrential rain to the entire area. General Maritz now in command of the besieging forces around Okiep was determined to carry on the fight at all costs. He had given orders to his men to build a gun with which to project dynamite bombs into Okiep, but this idea was not a success because each attempt to fire the piece resulted in the death of several Boers when the weapon blew up. Nevertheless, Maritz continued his plan to take the town and the valuable copper mines. While the Boers tightened their grip on Okiep more heliograph messages were sent by Colonel Cooper to assure Shelton he was pressing on.

More fog had now descended on the mountain and settled just above the valley below, thus making early morning 'helio' signalling impossible. The only method of contact was by the brave runners.

The Boers continued intensive sniping from all sides of the besieged town making movement within the garrison extremely difficult. The Crow's Nest and eastern ridges were keeping up a sustained fire, which was answered by the Okiep garrison. Okiep's nine pounder field gun was shelling the areas from which the heaviest fire appeared to be coming. This weapon was of considerable value to the garrison for without it and the two Maxim machine guns, the odds against Okiep would have been much greater.

The thick fog suddenly cleared, the sun came out and communication by heliograph was resumed. At 9.30am on the 28th Colonel Cooper sent another signal to Colonel Shelton:

"NN April 27th Sorry fog interfered with signals yesterday. Had a try to get into Steinkopf on Friday, but hope to get in there today. Probably my advance make enemy more alert round you. Be very careful Boers don't rush you. Keep me well informed of all news about enemy. You have never yet told me who was responsible for surrender of **CONCORDIA** Please do so, as inquiry must be held. **Smuts came in yesterday**"

CHAPTER 12

GENERAL VAN DEVENTER OPPOSES COLONEL COOPER

With General Smuts' arrival at Klipfontein to begin his historic journey to Vereeniging, there had been much speculation among Colonel Cooper's men, and the British generally, whether the Boers might now withdraw from Okiep. Their question was soon answered when an advanced party from Cooper's column suddenly came under heavy fire from the surrounding hills. Luckily none of the British soldiers were killed in this incident, but two were slightly wounded, and they withdrew at once. When news of this skirmish reached Cooper his hopes of an early end to the conflict faded and he realised the Boers were still determined to resist him. He therefore decided to launch his main attack against General Van Deventer. Reinforcements had arrived consisting of two companies of the 4th Battalion of the East Surrey Regiment and two companies of the 2nd Battalion Royal Fusiliers under the command of Captain Wolsely. Ironside's field guns were in position waiting for the order to fire. The Duke of Edinburgh's Own Volunteers were also part of the force.

All was now ready - men, horses, guns and ammunition - and at first light on 28th April, Colonel Cooper gave the order to fix bayonets. The guns opened fire and the relief force began to advance towards the Boer positions at Steinkopf. The column continued to advance, supported by Ironside's guns, and the effective fire of the Artillery was forcing the Boers to fall back to more secure positions. They re-grouped quickly and continued to oppose the column's advance. A Squadron of the 5th Lancers waited for their chance to charge any enemy who might be foolish enough to break away.

Four hours later the Boers were still holding Steinkopf which blocked the advance of Cooper's men. It was now obvious to Cooper he would have to think of another way of dislodging his enemy even at the risk of losing more of his men. While the column was halted he called for Lieutenant Ironside and his other officers in order to revise the plan of attack. However, unknown to Cooper, Ironside's field guns had already caused a large number of casualties among the Boers. The ground where some of the British troops had been halted was strewn with many dead Boers and horses, killed by shrapnel bursting above their heads while they were attempting to withdraw to higher ground. The battle continued throughout the day without any decision being reached, and at sunset Cooper decided to attack again at dawn. He sent word to all his troops in the front line to be vigilant during the night and prepare themselves for the forthcoming battle. His front line was now concentrated 500 yards from the entrance to Steinkopf where the Boers waited. Strict orders were given to all his troops not to attempt to advance further beyond this line. He sent the following situation report to Colonel Shelton by runner and a duplicate by helio, sent on the 29th April, reached Okiep the same day.

> "NP. Your O.K. of 24th and O.K. No 4 of 26th not yet received. Please report by Helio. Your White scouts have not yet arrived. Sorry to hear you have been **unwell**. Hope you are all right again. We had a fight with Van Deventer near **Steinkopf** yesterday. We had two killed and some other casualties but can account for 7 Boers killed and Van Deventer sent

From Col. A Cooper
Klipfontein
(Desp: 6am 30/4/02)

To Col Shelton
Ookiep
Klipfontein
29.4.02

NP. Your OK No 3 of 24th and OK No 4 of 26th not yet received. Please report by helio. Your white scouts have not yet arrived. Sorry to hear you have been unwell. Hope you are all right again. We had a fight with Van de Venter near Steinkopf yesterday We had two killed and some other casualties but can account for 7 Boers killed and Van de Venter sent in for a doctor to attend to his wounded this morning. Am expecting strong reinforcements of infantry today and shall push on at once. I will let you know by which way when I have started I have heard from White up to 22nd Have asked him HHHPB. NHXR

Heliograph message dated 29 April 1902 fromColonel Cooper.

AK7B7. RCVZI PYYFL CBQRP
VKCVR OHDXC XGXLX RKLTV
MPXDV SHHHH.

Apparently enemy were destroying
the mines at Concordia and Nababeep
yesterday. The railway from here to
Steinkopf badly damaged. Thanks for
information of Boer movements.

Hooper
Colonel
Comdg N.7.7.

Duplicate sent by helio 29.4.02
Received in Ookiep same day.

Page 2 of heliograph message.

in for a Doctor to attend to his wounded this morning. Am expecting strong reinforcements of infantry to-day and shall push on at once. I will let you know by which way when I have started. I have heard from White up to 22nd. Have asked him HHHPB. PHHXR. AKFBF. RCVZI. PYYFL. ETC. (5 letter code)

"Apparently enemy were destroying the mines at CONCORDIA and NABABEEP yesterday. The railway from here to Steinkopf badly damaged.
Thanks for information of BOER movements.

H. Cooper Colonel Commanding NFF"

The runner was a local coloured scout who knew the area well and was skilled in trekking and moving under cover quickly but it was going to take him three days and nights to reach his destination. His journey was most dangerous but he arrived safely.

In Okiep, the garrison and the civilian population were still under heavy pressure from General Maritz and his troops, although Colonel Shelton was able to repel any attempt by the Boers to advance too close to the town. Water continued to be in good supply and altogether the general food situation was fairly good and in accordance with Shelton's plan, system of rationing, all were catered for in the besieged town. His ammunition reserve was also adequate although he was getting short of shells for his field gun.

It was now the twenty-sixth day of the Siege and the garrison began to doubt whether they would ever be relieved by Cooper's men. The relief column was still held up at Steinkopf, fighting against Van Deventer. During this period of anxiety the firing from the surrounding hills increased and it seemed that a determined attack was about to be launched. The blockhouses and the field gun were returning the enemy fire and the noise of the battle was deafening. At the height of the action Captain Lutwyche of the Royal Warwicks decided to leave his position under what cover he could find and examine bullet holes in the side of a blockhouse - just exactly what he was looking for will remain a mystery - but as he crawled out of his trench he was spotted by a Boer sniper. Lutwyche had just reached the outer wall of the blockhouse when the sniper opened fire hitting him twice in the stomach. He was immediately given covering fire by his men in the north blockhouse who went out to bring him in. First aid was applied but did little for Lutwyche who was now unconscious from loss of blood. Colour Sergeant Stevens, realising his Captain was getting weaker, made his way to the hospital to get Dr. Howard and a stretcher. Lutwyche was taken back to the hospital under fire from the Boers, but luckily no one was hit, and following an immediate operation and the skill of Dr. Howard, Lutwyche's life was saved. Colour Sergeant Stevens, who had shown great bravery in bringing in his wounded officer had done so under constant enemy fire, but his reward was only a mention in despatches.

At 10am on the 30th April, Colonel Cooper sent a heliograph message to Shelton which had been delayed because there had been no sun on the previous day. This read:

"NS Your message received. Do what I can to help you, hope infantry reinforcements will reach me to-night."

Shelton was relieved to learn that further reinforcements were on their way to join Colonel Cooper, but the relief column had still not broken through the Boer defences at Steinkopf.

He considered it was now just a matter of time before the commando units were pushed back along the line towards Okiep and he realised that the more pressure Cooper put on the Boers, the greater was the likelihood of a rushed attack on the garrison. He acted swiftly, and ordered all officers and NCO's on the outer and inner defences to be vigilant and to report all movements of the enemy from the hills to the left and right of Okiep and also from the northern direction.

Later that morning Colonel Cooper sent a further Helio message to Colonel Shelton.

> "Copy of yours O.K. No 3 of 24th and original O.K. 44 of the 26th have reached me, also scouts Tallack and Stanway. Do not be alarmed at enemy's attempt to make dynamite gun. Cleverest men in the world have failed up to present time in inventing anything to fire dynamite. Please try and get these messages through to Colonel White at Garies. Message begins NQ April 29th your 22nd received. Much obliged for information I am concentrated here trying to get through Steinkopf which is occupied by Van Deventer. Am expecting strong reinforcements of infantry. HHHPN. HXRKF. BFRCV. ZFPHY. BQNCV. RPVKC. VROHD. XCXGX. LXRKL. TVMPX. DVSHH. Let me know your movements. I am in Heliograph communication with O'OKiep. Smuts came in and left for Cape Town on 26th. Van Deventer has sent in for doctor to attend his wounded after yesterday's fight at Steinkopf. Judging by smoke enemy is destroying mines at Concordia and Nababeep, and has seriously damaged railway between here and O'OKiep. N.Q April 29th Shelton reports Boer reinforcements reached Concordia from Upington - strength unknown - Langelaager at Silverfontein 40 miles S.E. of O'OKiep where large convoy had moved - where convoy came from not said and 50 Boers with 250 horses at Rietfontein 30 miles S.E. of O'OKiep. Message ends. Scouts Harris and Beck arrived here at midday. Detachment of Royal Fusiliers reached me last night - rest coming.
> H. Cooper Colonel"

Confirmed by runner to Okiep - then sent by Shelton to Colonel White in Garies.

The message was received by Shelton who was awaiting a further attack by dynamite bombers, and once again there was intensive sniping from the hills which continued throughout the day, answered, as always, by the garrison's blockhouse system and the men in the open trenches. While the Okiep garrison was preventing the Boers from advancing any further towards the town, Colonel Cooper's relief column was poised for an all-out attack on Van Deventer's position at Steinkopf.

Cooper's relief column began to advance on Steinkopf expecting fierce resistance, but they were surprised to find only a few snipers who opened fire as soon as the troops were within range. They were acting as a form of rearguard to Van Deventer's main force which, unknown to Cooper, had withdrawn from Steinkopf during the night and early hours of that morning. Lieutenant Ironside's field guns silenced many of the riflemen although the Boers were still shooting at the column until late that evening and hampering its advance.

Colonel Cooper realised that the enemy was withdrawing from Steinkopf but he was still very wary and expected a major counter-attack at any time. With this in mind he sent another heliograph message to Shelton;

> "Glad you are well. Enemy reported to have abandoned Steinkopf. Am pressing on this night to help you. Goodnight."

This message was received in Okiep at 4.45pm. The dates and time of each communication were vitally important to both the Commanding Officers because the situation for either of them could change drastically within a very short time.

Supplies of food, water and ammunition were being sent up the railway line now in a continuous flow, and this enabled the troops of the relief column to replenish necessary items as they advanced. Each train carried as much as possible along the line to Anenous where the supplies were loaded on mules and horses to be conveyed to the front line. Much forage was needed and this was running low at one stage of the campaign. Urgent telegrams were sent to Cape Town via the Royal Navy and the food arriving for the animals was despatched to the various posts where it was awaited. The Boers were withdrawing from Steinkopf towards Okiep to reinforce General Maritz who was keeping up the pressure on the garrison and its inhabitants. At 7.15pm, on the evening of the 30th April, another flag of truce was seen waving in the distance to the north of the town - the Boers who were pushing a trolley along the railway which ran into the town were allowed to approach, but were halted some distance from the outer trenches while Lieutenant Anstey went forward to find out what the Boers wanted. General Maritz had send in one of the garrison's black soldiers from the Okiep Town Guard who had been badly wounded about a week before in the fighting around the main blockhouses. A letter written in High Dutch and addressed to Shelton was handed to Lieutenant Anstey. Somehow Lieutenant Anstey and his CO felt there was something wrong and in fact this letter was a trick thought up by Maritz, in order to find out whether or not the railway line into the Okiep town centre was intact. He calculated that a massive quantity of dynamite, if exploded in the town, would compel the defenders to surrender. His plan was to load a truck attached to the Pioneer Engine with as much dynamite as it would hold and then run it into the town where it would explode with devastating results. (The Pioneer engine, which was captured by the Boers when Concordia surrendered, was normally used by the Namaqua Copper Company to convey copper ore from the mines to Port Nolloth.) Immediately after the explosion, Maritz and his men would attack the town and overrun the garrison, killing as many of the troops as possible.

*The decoy letter sent by Maritz prior to despatching the dynamite truck
and engine night of 30th April/1st May*

Translation: *We send you one of your wounded to Okiep with Dr Möller and
Mr Roberts. Dr Möller has to go out so much that he cannot give him the
proper attention his wounds require.*

However, General Ben Bouwer who was also operating with General Smuts' troops against Okiep, considered that this was an unacceptable ruthless operation. He knew there were many women and children in Okiep and in his opinion they had to be considered. In addition, he knew there were a great many Copper Mines under the town and large areas would subside following such a massive explosion. The dynamite train was then made ready but before it was despatched General Bouwer inspected the load to ensure there were no detonators in the cases of dynamite, though it is doubtful whether this would have had any effect on the planned outcome. Dynamite is a dangerous substance which will explode on receiving a sharp knock, even without detonators and there was every chance of this happening, whether by rifle or derailment. Nevertheless General Bouwer's intention was entirely laudable for he hoped to save the lives of women and children in the town.

The Pioneer engine and truck were made ready. The engine's task was to shunt the truck along the railway line which ran upwards towards Braakputs Junction and Okiep, and then into the town centre. Colonel Shelton had previously erected a strong barbed wire fence across the railway line. Some of this wire was attached to the points at the Braakputs Junction.

At 5am the Pioneer, pushing its truck loaded with 70 cases of dynamite rumbled off into the darkness with sparks flying from its smoke stack. It came to the points at the Braakputs junction and suddenly the truck heeled over and left the line, throwing the cases of dynamite onto the ground where they ignited in a tremendous blaze. The Pioneer had hit the wire fence with great force, causing the derailment of the truck.

Gallagher - one of the Irishmen who was serving with General Bouwer - had fitted several lengths of fuse to the dynamite which he knew would ignite it when it reached its destination. The brilliance of the flames from the dynamite lit up the surrounding

The 5th Lancers on the march.

180

countryside as though it was daylight and Okiep was illuminated. The Boers then realised that their attempt at blowing up the garrison had failed. Shelton ordered the garrison to stand to as it seemed the Boers were bound to take advantage of the confusion and attack. General Maritz, who had been watching the progress of the locomotive and the dynamite truck was disappointed to see he had not achieved the result he had planned. Colonel Shelton had already been warned that an attempt of this nature might be made, and had ordered his officers in the outer defences not to fire on the locomotive or the truck for fear of hitting the dynamite and exploding it. Even at a considerable distance such an explosion would certainly have been catastrophic for Okiep. There was always the danger that it would have caused automatic explosions amongst his reserve ammunition. Fortunately, his barbed wire fence had saved Okiep.

At dawn the garrison troops were able to see the Pioneer locomotive still on the line with the truck on its side. It was now Okiep's 'trophy of war' and Shelton ordered his marksmen to cover the engine should the Boers approach it. During the morning his scouts reported that they were retiring from their positions on the railway line. He also heard that some Boers were withdrawing from Steinkopf moving in a south-easterly direction and were not taking any prisoners with them. On hearing this Colonel Shelton became confident that Colonel Cooper and his men were succeeding in driving the Boers out of Steinkopf.

CHAPTER 13

THE FINAL STAGES

On the morning of the 2nd May the situation was virtually unchanged. The Boers were withdrawing slowly towards the south leaving a large force to continue the siege of Okiep, and many were still waiting in the hills to engage the troops of the relief force as they advanced. The outer defences of the garrison were still under sniper fire which also caused casualties in the town. General Maritz knew his attempt to blow up Okiep with the dynamite truck could not be repeated, and by now there had been much killing and wounding on both sides with little result. At Nababeep other commando units were creating havoc and damaging as much property as possible in the vicinity. Although Colonel Cooper's men were pressing on, the commando units were dispersing in order to re-group as a larger force. The determined efforts of the Boers were gradually being made ineffective by Cooper's men and the garrison of Okiep which had held out bravely against superior forces. Many of the Boers were now becoming disheartened, knowing they might have to withdraw from the area having lost many of their comrades in arms and Smuts had now left them and was on his way to the peace talks at Vereeniging. It now seemed unlikely they would gain a much better deal for their families despite the great sacrifices they had made. Throughout the Transvaal, Orange Free State and the Cape Colony were thousands of graves on the veld, little or no cattle, farmhouses in ruins, and the Boer women and children scattered far and wide. Approximately 26,000 of them had died in the British concentration camps, originally intended to protect them from hostilities.

Maritz now knew he could not take Okiep but he could not bring himself to order his men to withdraw towards Grootkou and the South-Eastern District where he thought there were only a few British troops.

Colonel Cooper's column was drawing nearer and had now occupied Steinkopf and an advanced guard was moving into the country ahead. Cooper continued to keep in close contact with Shelton, for example:

"From Colonel Cooper   Colonel Shelton, O'OKiep

"N.U. May 1 Your three messages of yesterday are to hand. Sorry to hear Captain Lutwyche's wound hope he is doing well. Van Deventer succeeded to command on departure of Smuts. He left Steinkopf towards Paardegat evening of 29th. Understand Maritz is commanding round O'OKiep. Steinkopf evacuated during night 29th/30th. Hope to occupy it today. I gave Phillips Cashier of Copper Company permit from Port Nolloth to Cape Town. Anxious to get hold of Phillips Senior Bowers of Hartebeestefontein and Cooper of Contres came in yesterday and are being forwarded to Port Nolloth for disposal by magistrate Brecker and Schleder will be similarly treated when caught. I note your wish about promotion and will talk it over when we meet. We send you papers by every runner our last one 29 March.

"A Parker Capt. 5th Lancers SO N77 Original by helio 1.5.02
by runner from Steinkopf 2.5.02"

The news from Cooper was most encouraging for Shelton who was now feeling confident that his garrison would be liberated by the relief column. Nevertheless Concordia and Springbok were still strongly held by the Boers with British field intelligence reporting that more reinforcements were still joining the commandos from the Upington area. The situation was by no means favourable for Shelton even though he anticipated a break through by Cooper at any hour. Captain Allan Borchards (SO) who was in telephone communication with him had received a short message from the signal station at Klipfontein stating that troops of the 7th Battalion Royal Fusiliers had reinforced Colonel Cooper during the previous night and were moving up the line to join him.

The situation had changed little for the inhabitants of Okiep. The Boers maintained their constant fire from the eastern hills. Communication with the outside world was still by heliograph or native runner. Shelton also had his mounted scouts. These black runners, who were familiar with the local area, were of the greatest asset to Shelton and every credit must be given to them for their splendid devotion to these dangerous tasks. The exchange of messages between Cooper and Shelton was increasing every day as the relief column drew closer to Okiep. Cooper had received news of the Okiep garrison's sortie against the commando and this prompted him to send a longer communication to Okiep, feeling sure it would boost the garrison's morale.

"Very glad to hear that instead of Boers attacking you - you were able to attack them last night (1st May) with such success that today they are trekking towards Springbok. I am afraid that owing to scarcity of water and lack of transport I shall not come up with them again before reaching O'OKiep. My advanced posts Royal Fusiliers and Cape Police are at 69th mile stone near Paardegat. This evening and with ordinary luck a flying column of 5th Lancers, Imperial Yeoman RFA and Royal Fusiliers, ought to reach you on the 4th or 5th inst. Be on the look out for them, and they will require Rations and Forage. Numbers about 350 men and 200 horses and 200 mules. Lt. Col. Callwell RA will be in command, so be on the lookout. Have you got any news of White? If you have a chance let him know that my advance depots will be at Paardegat. The remainder of the Royal Fusiliers has arrived at Port Nolloth and should join me here tomorrow. Hoping to see you in the course of the next few days. I hope Capt. Lutwyche and the remainder of the wounded both men and women are doing well.

Signed Col. H. Cooper, Commg. N.F.F."

This was cheering news for Shelton and the garrison as the word spread quickly around the besieged town, arousing determination to defy the Boers by opening fire immediately any movement in the hills was seen. The general situation around the Copper Mining area had changed. Colonel Cooper had occupied Steinkopf and was pushing on, at the same time advising Shelton not to be alarmed about the availability of dynamite because a great deal of it had been left at Steinkopf and very little local damage had been done.

While General Smuts was on his way to Vereeniging to attend the peace conference, Colonel White had broken out from Garies, having joined up with a small supply convoy of arms and ammunition which had been sent out by Shelton. Maritz was maintaining his watch on Okiep and had received no orders to do otherwise, although General Van Deventer's men were now pulling back from their positions south of Steinkopf and his scouts were riding into the open spaces in the eastern areas where they had a better chance of avoiding the British Army patrols. The last of Cooper's reinforcements had arrived at Port Nolloth and were making their way along the railway line to join him. They left the heavily defended Port to protect itself, should there be a sudden change in strategy by the Boers. However, at this particular stage of the conflict no peace had been signed and hostilities were continuing over a wide area with even more determined aggression between the two opposing forces.

Cooper's main force had successfully reached the 69th mile stone on the railway line where they set up a temporary but well guarded supply point. They realised the Boers were still in a position to make a determined attack which could create havoc and even cut the railway link. The relief column was heavily outnumbered by the re-grouped commando which could be deployed by Maritz or Van Deventer. With this in mind, Cooper ordered his men to be extremely vigilant especially at night, when anywhere along the railway line could be attacked.

CHAPTER 14

THE BOERS WITHDRAW

On 29th April, Colonel White and his men met a convoy of supplies sent out by Shelton many days earlier. It was through White's determination and strong will that he saved his men and all their arms when cut off near Garies. The welcome supplies were distributed among his soldiers who were extremely short of fresh rations and water. Their horses and mules were given forage while a ring of guards covered the surrounding area. Colonel White's men and animals ate and drank well during the welcome break from fighting General Maritz' men. As the immediate vicinity was reported clear of Boers by White's scouts, he decided to send back to Okiep for orders. He waited for news from Shelton while his men and horses took a much needed rest.

Although Shelton was now optimistic and felt the relief of Okiep would be realised soon - he still had the enemy at the front door, and he was taking no chances, in case General Maritz had some idea of launching a final attack. Many of the Boers were in two minds now about attacking the Okiep defenders. They knew General Smuts was on his way to a Peace Conference with the British and were still uncertain of the outcome and naturally this held them back. On the 2nd May 1902 the general situation was precarious for all the commando units that had fought so hard and travelled great distances with their original leader - it was a bitter blow for them to accept a compromise which might result in the loss of their independence from the British.

At 3pm on 3rd May 1902 Shelton received the following heliograph message from Colonel Cooper in Steinkopf:

> "Your despatch O.K. No 5 of 30th April received by runner this morning. Colonel Caldwells flying column has left to join you. Royal Fusiliers expected here to-morrow morning. For some time to come Steinkopf will be railhead. All conveyance between Steinkopf and O'OKiep being done by wagon. We will probably come by Rattlepoort."

For the first time since the beginning of the siege the Boers did not open fire on Okiep. Many of them were now waiting to join Van Deventer's men who, some days previously had opposed Cooper's column near Steinkopf. They had split up into small groups with the idea of joining the main commando, which had been attacking Okiep Mining Headquarters but the 5th Lancers were reconnoitring the area around Steinkopf and saw some of these Boer parties. They gave chase, but the Boers escaped. Many of them had already slipped away during the night, and were making for Grootkou in the east, where the commando had a remote depot. They were joined by the original Smuts' commando which was evacuating Concordia. There were hundreds of Boer commando now riding together, hoping to evade the British Army patrols that were searching for them.

Colonel Shelton in Okiep received news of the withdrawal of the Boers and allowed some of the women and children to return to their houses which had been empty for over a month.

It was now clear that the commando units were retiring from the Copper Mining area via Nababeep, Concordia and Springbokfontein. Colonel Callwell, leading a flying column of 5th Lancers, Imperial Yeomanry, RFA and Royal Fusiliers, was making his way down the railway line to Rattlepoort, and it was now only a matter of hours before the relief vanguard would enter Okiep and raise the siege. When Shelton heard that Concordia was clear of the Boers he wondered what had happened to the British prisoners captured by Smuts and Maritz but, unknown to him, Lieutenants MacIntyre and Dorrington of the Namaqualand Border Scouts, with other prisoners of war, had been released and left behind in Concordia. All were in good health and had been treated well by the Boers. The prisoners of war captured by the Boers and now released were required to give the Resident Magistrate affidavits which recorded their treatment while in Boer captivity, adding general information about the Boers and those inhabitants of Namaqualand who had decided to fight with the Boers against the British, or assist them in any way they felt necessary.

While Colonel Shelton was awaiting the arrival of the relief column, he issued an order that all natives from the vicinity should now be allowed to return to their homes and huts, although there was still a risk of further sniping be Boer marksmen, many of whom were still positioned outside the town and waiting for orders to withdraw.

Shelton soon had to qualify his permission for women, children and servants to return to their homes because he was told they were wandering about in the open and showing lights after dark. He issued orders that no person would be allowed to step outside the laager at night, adding that all private houses must be vacated at dusk after which 'no lights' must be seen in them.

The exterior and interior lines of defence were maintained and no one was allowed to leave his post without permission from his commanding officer.

POST OFFICE TELEGRAPHS.
CAPE OF GOOD HOPE.

No. of Message. 2

Dated Stamp of

3 / 5 / 02

Handed in at _____ at _____ M.

Received here at 3 P M.

Delivering Office.

From	To
Col Cooper Steinkopf	Col Shelton O'Kiep

NZ May 3rd Your despatch
OK No 5 of 30th
received by runner this morning.
Col Calwell's flying column has
left to join you Royal
Fusiliers expected here tomorrow morning.
For some time to come
Steinkopf will be railhead all
Conveyance between Steinkopf and O'Kiep
being done by wagon. We
will probably come by Ratelpoort

Colonel Cooper's progress

187

CHAPTER 15

THE RELIEF OF OKIEP

The night of the 2nd/3rd May passed quietly and without incident, giving many in Okiep a much needed rest. The soldiers and all volunteers had been in the trenches for over a month. At daybreak the garrison awaited more sniping from the ridges, but none came. The sun rose bringing a welcome glow of warmth from behind the eastern hills. The Okiep garrison remained on full alert as water and rations were issued for breakfast. News had come from Shelton's HQ that the vanguard of the relief column might be arriving in Okiep on the morning of the 4th or 5th May. Captain Freeland RA was ordered by Shelton to select a camp site for it, near the railway, to facilitate the transport of supplies.

While the garrison troops enjoyed the break from fighting, the advanced guard of Colonel Cooper's relief column was entering Rattlepoort on the railway. It halted at 11.00am and the units dispersed to mount sentries and lookouts in case the enemy was concealed nearby. They remained at Rattlepoort and waited for Cooper's main force to join them.

Four of the men of Cooper's column who were killed in the fight against General Van Deventer's troops at Steinkopf are buried at Klipfontein between the Anenous pass and Steinkopf. They are:
Cpl H. McLauchlin, Pte J.B. Parr, Pte R.A. Plim - Imperial Yeomanry and Pte W. Armstrong - Duke of Edinburgh's Own Volunteer Regiment.

It was late in the evening of 3rd May when the first troops of the main column began to arrive at Ratelpoort. Colonel Cooper ordered them to wait for dawn on the 4th as he felt there was no point in pressing on through the night, with all the difficulties and dangers it could bring.

The largest force of Boers had now withdrawn to the south and east and were joining other commando units. They had not given up the fight and were still determined to resist any British attempts to capture them. The Boers now riding again on the veld knew nothing of the progress of the peace talks but they assumed all must be going well because the well-organised Boer intelligence service had reported that Smuts had been welcomed with great cordiality by General French.

An historic heliograph message, signalling the virtual end of the Siege of Okiep was sent by Colonel Cooper to Colonel Shelton on 3rd May:

"From Colonel Cooper, Steinkopf
To Colonel Shelton

"N.N.A 3rd May. Your W.S. 19 of 3rd May received. Congratulations on your anxieties being relieved. Unless opposed Lt Colonel Callwell will be at Rattlepoort this evening and will be with you tomorrow. You will have

*The graves of the four soldiers killed in
action near Steinkopf.*

to feed him and his horses. Royal Fusiliers are to strengthen your garrison mounted troops camp outside town. Hope to be with you tomorrow afternoon."

At 7.30am the morning of the 4th May the advanced guard of Colonel Cooper's relief column was seen in the distance by the look-outs on the Okiep exterior line of defence. Lieutenant Anstey at once gave the order for six rockets to be sent up at intervals of ten seconds indicating the approach of the column.

Seen through binoculars, Cooper's men appeared more clearly - first a few soldiers, then many, as they advanced towards the outer line of defence. It was soon possible to see them with the naked eye, and a great roar went up from the men of the garrison. The cheering continued and was heard in the interior defence lines and by the civilians in the town. The reaction was electric, the town's children ran as fast as they could towards the outer defences, the women and girls went with them, shouting and screaming, some even crying with joy - all in a frantic race to greet the relieving heroes. In the general

189

pandemonium no-one cared whether or not there were any Boer marksmen around the hills, as more and more of Cooper's men came in sight. It was a day that should not be forgotten in the military and civil history of South Africa and the British Empire. As the relieving troops rode and marched into the town the siege of Okiep came to an end.

In arriving with his men at the northern outposts of the town, Colonel Caldwell raised the siege, which had lasted for a month, and Colonel Shelton and his officers went to greet him and his men. There was a great deal of handshaking and kissing as the women and girls embraced the troops in an emotional atmosphere. The sentries, however, were still maintaining a careful watch on the surrounding ridges. At 12 noon Colonel Cooper arrived in Okiep with his staff, and being senior to Colonel Shelton, assumed command of the Namaqualand District.

The HQ of the NFF moved from Steinkopf to Okiep later that day. After a long conversation with Colonel Shelton, Colonel Cooper made some immediate administrative appointments. In addition to his duties as Administrator of Namaqualand Colonel Shelton was, for the present, to act as Commandant, Okiep. Colonel Donald CB commanding the Royal Fusiliers was appointed Commandant of Steinkopf. Major Logan RA was appointed as Base Commandant of Port Nolloth. It was now considered safe to allow all the refugees who were residing north of a line drawn from Okiep to Ramans Drift, and from Springbok through Komaggas and Spektakel to Buffels River Mouth, to return to their homes. Travel permits were signed by the Civil Commissioner as Martial Law was still in force, and the British Military Authorities were controlling all movements in Namaqualand District. Many of the women and children had now returned to their homes which had been struck by rifle fire during the height of the siege. Work began to clear up any external damage to property as well as the inside of the houses. Colonel Shelton was trying to maintain a complete roster of sentry duties and at the same time draw up a plan to compensate anyone in the town who had suffered loss or damage during the siege.

The copper mines were the first consideration. Although in Okiep none of the mines had been damaged by the Boers during the fighting, at Nababeep there was a different tale to tell. A great deal of mining machinery, blown up by dynamite was beyond repair and the damage done to mine shafts made reconstruction difficult. The cost estimated to be thousands of pounds would have to be found from somewhere. As no work could be carried out in the copper mines during the siege of Okiep there was a great loss of production for the Cape Copper Company. The Board of Directors in London was already meeting to estimate the total loss, and this would be increased by the severe damage to the Cape Copper Company railway at Steinkopf, Klipfontein and other locations along the line. New rails and sleepers as well as specialised mining equipment would have to be purchased in England and shipped out to Port Nolloth.

The area began to settle down to a more peaceful atmosphere but initially it was difficult for the inhabitants to realise they were no longer living in daily fear of their lives, and it was some time before the civilians and the Town Guards and Border Scouts were able to adjust to peace conditions.

Out on the open veld, stray horses were roaming around looking for food and they had to be rounded up. Dead bodies, partly decomposed, were still lying where they had fallen because there had been no time to bury them. They were Boers or volunteers who had fought bravely during the long war against the British, and many graves had to be located. This vast area today has few memorials to those who died and the war left deep scars in the minds of the Boers and their families for many generations.

The Thanksgiving Service after the raising of the Siege. The entire garrison and community of Okiep attended plus many from Nababeep, Concordia and Springbokfontein.

Okiep Garrison on farewell parade

CHAPTER 16

COLONEL SHELTON SAYS FAREWELL TO OKIEP AND NAMAQUALAND

When the celebrations for the relief of Okiep were well under way, various messages and congratulations began to arrive for Colonel Shelton and his garrison. They came from Colonel Cooper and his men in the relief column, From General Settle in Cape Town, Colonel Haig and General French. There was also one from Lord Kitchener who mentioned in his despatches the successful defence of the important copper mining district and its eventual relief from the besieging Boer forces. Shelton knew that his task, for which he had been specially selected by the Cape Governor, Alfred Milner, was virtually over and it only remained for him to ensure a safe return to the houses and farms of everyone who had taken refuge in Okiep during the emergency.

It was now the 5th May, and peace for South Africa was only three weeks away. The first meeting between the representatives of the two Boer republics and the British, held in the town of Vereeniging on the border of the Transvaal and the Orange Free State was held on 15th May 1902. General Smuts had prepared his proposals for the peace terms which he was to argue with the British delegates headed by Sir Alfred Milner. He also had his own ideas on the conditions for a peace settlement.

At first there was a lot of heated discussion revolving round an 'oath of allegiance' which the burgers would be asked to sign in order to establish a constitution for South Africa. This embraced such important aspects as the Dutch and English languages, the rebels who had fought against the British and the surrender of all Boer forces wherever they might be.

Meanwhile, as the talks slowly progressed, Colonel Shelton had been touring his area up to Port Nolloth on the west coast to see for himself the damage caused by the Boers to the railway and in the towns. In many areas the destruction was considerable, and the cost of it would have to be calculated for compensation. Luckily, the wooden viaducts at Anenous were still intact, thanks to Lieutenant Moffat and the men of the 2nd Battalion of the Namaqualand Border Scouts, who had prevented the Boers from destroying them with dynamite. The railway was in fact now complete, all the repairs having been carried out by the Royal Engineers. At the finish of Shelton's 'little tour', he made notes which were to be included in a general report to Colonel Cooper.

The surrender of Concordia was to be fully investigated and a General Court Martial, convened under the orders of General French, to try those involved, was to be held on the 23rd June at Okiep. Colonel Shelton had also compiled a list of official casualties. (Appendix A.)

Colonel Shelton circulated his farewell message to everyone in Okiep and the surrounding district.

"To the garrison of O'OKiep etc.,

"In relinquishing command of the Namaqualand District I desire to convey to the Officers and N.C.O's and all men who have served under me during the past eighteen months - my highest praise and appreciation of the splendid service rendered by all ranks and of the valuable assistance I have received by all during the period of my command.

"I can find no words to express my admiration of the conduct of the troops of the O'OKiep garrison throughout the harassing and trying month of the Siege, nor that would do justice to the **Courage**, **Endurance** and **Cheerfulness** displayed not only by the troops but by the whole community. My warm thanks are due to Major Dean, Major Evans and the Officers of the Namaqualand Town Guard Battalion for their loyal support and the splendid example they set their men.

"To the officers of my staff Major Dean, Captains Freeland, Mitchell and MacDonald, Dr Howard and Mr. Vrolik I offer my heartfelt gratitude for all the assistance they have invariably and unfailingly rendered me.

"I am also indebted to the officers of the 'Cape Garrison Artillery' and 1st and 2nd Battalions of the Namaqualand Border Scouts for the good work done by them at all times.

"I particularly wish to acknowledge with gratitude the valuable assistance I have always received from not only the Superintendent and officials of the Cape Copper Company at **O'OKiep** and **Port Nolloth** but also from the employees of the Company generally.

"My thanks are due to the following gentlemen who have been of the greatest assistance to me - Messrs. Van Renen, CC and RM Howe Brownm, RM Captain Hodge, NBS deputy Administrator and the Revds. D Schierhoudt, Locke and Hewitt and Dr. Thomas.

"To my colleague during the past year, Lieut. Colonel White, I wish to convey my warmest thanks for his ever ready and kind help, advice and hearty co-operation.

"In saying 'Goodbye' to one and all I desire to reiterate my thanks for the great kindness and attention extended to me by all and wish **LUCK**, **HAPPINESS**, and **PROSPERITY** to Namaqualand and everyone in it.

Signed Lt.Col. W.A.D. Shelton
Willington Augustus David Shelton
3rd Battalion The Queens Royal West Surrey Regiment
7th July, 1902."

Shelton wrote a report to General French in which he said he wanted to testify to the splendid behaviour of all ranks of the defending forces under his command throughout the 30 day siege "Where all did so well it would be invidious to draw comparisons. A magnificent and cheerful spirit prevailed throughout the siege and it never seemed to enter one's head that the result would be otherwise than as it had turned out". "The Cape Garrison Artillery Gun Detachment, 9 pounder and Maxims under the command of Capt. Freeland, RA, undoubtedly on many occasions silenced the enemy's fire and arrested attack. The men of the 5th Battalion. (less than half a company) of the Royal Warwickshire Regt., behaved well while the soldier like qualities, fire discipline and endurance of all officers, N.C.O's and men of the Namaqualand Town Guard Batt. left nothing to be desired and did credit to the Civilian Army of the Cape Colony. The H.Q. Troops of the Namaqualand Border Scouts worked well in all capacities when and where required and the volunteers - both white and black behaved gallantly".

Colonel Shelton having relinquished his command to Colonel Cooper, made preparations to bid farewell to Namaqualand and return to Cape Town. The conference at Vereeniging had finally agreed on peace terms, largely in direct conversations between Kitchener and Smuts, but it was not until 31st May 1902 that a formal agreement ended hostilities and it was possible to begin rebuilding homes and properties which had been destroyed by the scorched earth policy throughout the Orange Free State, Transvaal and neighbouring areas in the Cape Colony. Compensation of £3,000,000 would be paid by the British tax payer as a contribution to this end, and large loans were offered to help re-establish the farmers and their live stock.

Generals Botha, De Wet and J.H. De la Rey visited England to negotiate further terms in respect of the loans with the British Government and they travelled to Britain on the same ship as Colonel Shelton. This is probably why Shelton travelled incognito and was not named in the first class passenger list of the *RMS Saxon*, owned by the Union Castle Line. The *Saxon* left Cape Town on 30th July, bound for Southampton via Madeira, and reached England in mid-August. There was no official reception for Shelton on the Quay, but instead his wife and two children were there to meet him. As the excited crowds gathered to catch a glimpse of the Boer party , Colonel Shelton and his family slipped quietly away to the train which took them to London.

On the 8th December 1902 Colonel Shelton was notified by the War Office that he had been awarded the Distinguished Service Order, and that King Edward VII had graciously agreed to present it to him at Buckingham Palace on the 18th December 1902 at 11.30 in the morning. A fitting reward for his services in South Africa.

On the 4th May 1903, the first anniversary of the raising of the siege of Okiep, he resigned his commission and settled down to enjoy the remaining years of his life with his family. He died six years later on the 14th June 1909 at Langford Hall in Essex. He was just 60, and was laid to rest in the graveyard of St. Giles Parish Church, Langford. He had completed a long and distinguished military career, which had culminated in the far of North-Western Cape Colony of South Africa. He never met his foe, General Jan Smuts, although from the tone of their letters to each other it was obvious there was mutual respect. Smuts lived on for more than forty years becoming an extremely popular international statesman and he died on the 11 September, 1950.

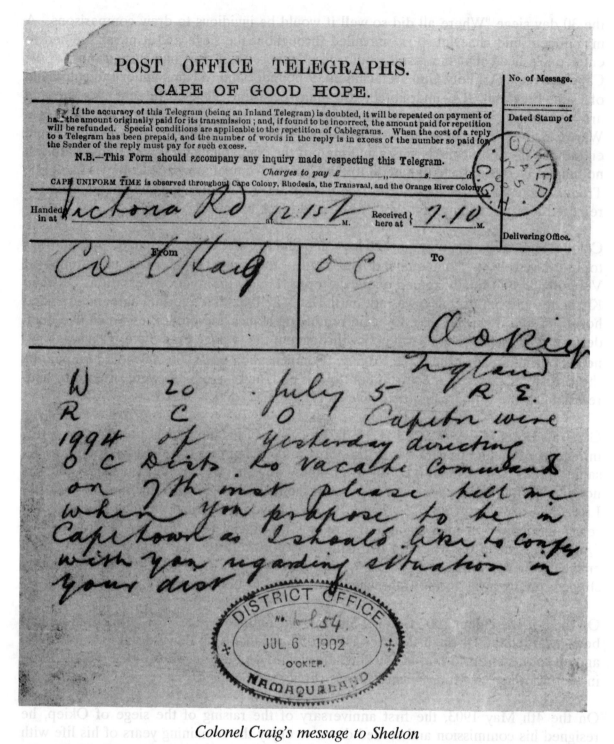

Colonel Craig's message to Shelton

Union Castle Line Passenger List Cover

*The Union Castle liner **Saxon** which brought Colonel Shelton to
England as well as the Boer delegation.*

R.M.S. "SAXON."
FIRST SALOON PASSENGERS.

Lord Alan Percy
Baron Pitner
Baroness Pitner
Master Pitner
Major-General Fitzroy Hart
General Dalfield
General Botha
Master Botha
General De la Rey
Mrs. De la Rey
General C. de Wet
Col. Chance
Col. Lambert
Col. Western
Major Sir A. Lushington
Major C Johnstone
Major Travers
Major Whittle
Major Everitt
Major Nickalls
Major Sitwell
Major Carter-Campbell
Major Johnson
Capt. Buller
Capt. Boone
Capt. Willoughby

Capt. Studd
Capt. L. G. Ionides
Capt. Bailey
Capt. McRae
Capt. MacLean
Capt. Mortey
Capt. R. S. Hunt
Capt. H. R. Lee
Capt. Cary
Capt. Irby
Capt. Wardlow
Lieut. Scarlett
Lieut. Wilcox Gower
Lieut. Wills
Lieut. Dugdale
Lieut. Jones
Lieut. Ewart
Lieut. Eupton
Lieut. Stewart
Lieut. Gavard
Lieut. Darrel
Lieut. The Hon. Baring
Lieut. M. Hodgson
Lieut. Mayalt
Lieut. A. Walker
Lieut. Dickson

R.M.S. "SAXON."
FIRST SALOON PASSENGERS.

Lieut. T. Cook
Lieut. Woods
Lieut. Elphinstone
Lieut. Forster
Lieut. R. G. Rawe
Lieut. J. Brande
Lieut. Phillips
Lieut. J. A. Armstrong
Lieut. Magee
Mr. B. Thomas
Dr. Stevenson
Mrs. S. G. Campbell
Miss Campbell
Master Campbell
Master Campbell
Master Campbell
Miss Adam
Miss Browne
Miss Burdon
Mrs. Douglas
Mr. A. May
Mrs. May
Mr. C. Wilson
Mrs. Wilson
Mr. Finch
Mr. Normand

Mrs. Normand
Mrs. Stent
Miss Stent
Miss Stent
Mrs. W. H. Gordon
Miss Gordon
Miss J. Gordon
Miss Gordon
Mrs. Walker
Master Walker
Mr. John Boyd
Mrs. E. H. Walton
Miss Walton
Miss D. Walton
Miss H. Walton
Mr. Max Silbermann
Mrs. Silbermann
Mrs. W. Thomson
Master Thomson
Miss Brewis
Mr. F. J. Horn
Mr. H. Mockford
Dr. Tilemann
Mr. Rees
Mr. W. E. Burmester
Mr. Quinn

The First Class passenger list

Boer prisioners awaiting a ship to take them to St. Helena Island.

Boers at Cape Town Docks.

Showing the obverse of the Cape Copper Company Medal.

British Graves on the veld.

So ends the story of the siege of Okiep, which records for the first time the campaign in Namaqualand. These military operations, covering one of the largest and most inhospitable districts in South Africa, were carried out by Colonel Shelton, assisted by Colonel White and troops of the 3rd Battalion of the Queens Royal Regiment, the 5th Battalion of the Royal Warwickshire Regiment, The Cape Town Highlanders, The Cape Garrison Artillery, local Cornish miner volunteers, the Okiep Town Guard, coloured Namaqualand Border Scouts and numerous civilians.

RETURN OF CASUALTIES OF O'OKIEP GARRISON

KILLED

Reconnoitring Patrol under command of Lieut. MacIntyre 1st N.B.S.
GROOTKAU. 31st March, 1902.

Trooper Stephanus Cloete	1st N.B.S.	Coloured
Trooper Johannes Cloete	" "	"
Trooper Manus Losper	" "	"
Trooper Johannes van Wyk	" "	"
Trooper William Golliat	" "	"
Trooper William Hollenbach	" "	"
Trooper William Klasse	" "	"
Trooper Jacobus Mulder	" "	"
Trooper Johannes Brandt	" "	"
Trooper Moses Cloete	" "	"

SPRINGBOKFONTEIN 1st April, 1902

Private R.J. Stewart N.T.G. Batt.	White
Volunteer H. van Coevoerden	"
Volunteer Tehart	Coloured

O'OKiep

8/4/02 Private Carolus Johannes	N.T.G. Batt.	Coloured
12/4/02 Private Samuel Richards	" "	White
12/4/02 Private Jacobus Arends	" "	Coloured
23/4/02 Volunteer Jantje Jantjes		"
28/4/02 Volunteer William Jantjes		"

Non-combatants

10/4/02 J Thomas	Male	Coloured
10/4/02 W Cloete	"	"
10/4/02 R de Klerk	Female	"

COMBATANTS WOUNDED   O'OKiep

(a) Officers

15/4/02 Lieut. T.S. Watkinson	1st N.B.S.	slightly
29/4/02 Capt. H. Lutwyche	5th R.War.Regt.	dangerously

(b) N.C.O.'s and men.

Date	Name	Role	Unit	Location/Colour
				GROOTKAU
31/3/02	Trooper J. Cloete		1st N.B.S.	Coloured
31/3/02	Trooper C. Cloete		" "	"
31/3/02	Trooper P. Cloete		" "	"
31/3/02	Trooper W. Brandt		" "	"
31/3/02	Trooper P. Cloete		" "	"
				SPRINGBOKFONTEIN
				White
1/4/02	D Cormack	Gaoler		"
1/4/02	O Ziegler	Chief Constable	D.M.P.	"
1/4/02	B Loynes	Trooper	"	"
1/4/02	J Juli	Constable		Coloured
1/4/02	John Kaffir	Volunteer		"
1/4/02	Trooper Cloete		2nd N.B.S.	"
1/4/02	W Obies	Volunteer		
				O'OKiep
8/4/02	Private P. Paine		N.T.G. Batt.	White
9/4/02	a/Bombdr Frankenberg		Cape Garr. Arty.	"
10/4/02	Private Henry Hein		2nd N.B.S.	Coloured
11/4/02	Private Jones		5th R.War Regt.	White
11/4/02	Private W Edin		" "	"
12/4/02	Private W van Book		N.T.G.B.	Coloured
12/4/02	Private Jacob Overtime		"	"
12/4/02	Private Jacob Frederick		"	"
13/4/02	Private Jim Paul		"	"
22/4/02	Sergt W W Townsend		"	"
23/4/02	Private G Magerman		"	"
23/4/02	Private H Bloem		"	"
23/4/02	P. Looper		Volunteer	"
24/4/02	J Wine		"	"
1/5/02	J Cloete		FID scout	"

NON-COMBATANTS

Date	Name		Colour
8/4/02	Klaas Pompey	Boy	Coloured
10/4/02	P Juli	"	"
10/4/02	Sarah Slane	Girl	"
10/4/02	N. Titys	Boy	"
11/4/02	J Cloete	Man	"
11/4/02	Mina Juli	Girl	Native
14/3/02	T Mbelini	Man	Coloured
14/3/02	K Ohlsonn	Girl	"
15/4/02	H Cloete	"	"
15/4/02	J. Isaacs	Boy	White
15/4/02	Annie Clacker	Girl	"
16/4/02	Jan Cloete	Man	Native

Date	Name		Race
18/4/02	John Cloete	"	Coloured
18/4/02	Andries Demara	"	"
19/4/02	Elsie Cloete	Girl	"
20/4/02	Fred Smith	Man	"
20/4/02	P Cloete	"	"
23/4/02	Kok Lace	"	"
27/4/02	Andries Darmara	"	"
1/5/02	Jacobus Portuin	"	"

PRISONERS

(a) Officers

		GROOTKAU	
31/3/02	Lieut. Wm. Macintyre	1st N.B.S.	
		SPRINGBOKFONTEIN	
1/4/02	Lieut. W. Dorrington	2ND N.B.S.	
		CONCORDIA	
4/4/02	Capt. G.G. Wrentmore	N.T.B. Batt.	
4/4/02	Lieut. S.F. Phillips	" "	
4/4/02	Lieut. Garland	" "	

(b) N.C.O.'s and men

GROOTKAU

31/3/02	N. 469 Trooper Gert Joseph	1st N.B.S.	Coloured
31/3/02	Trooper Van Renen	Cape Police	White
31/3/02	Trooper Wallace	" "	"

SPRINGBOKFONTEIN

4/4/02	No. 427 Sergt C Bond	N.T.B. Batt.	
4/4/02	No. 428 Sergt G.G. Mollet	" "	
4/4/02	No. 429 Sergt A Loynes	" "	
4/4/02	No. 431 Corpl C Magor	" "	
4/4/02	No. 430 Corpl W.H.White	" "	
4/4/02	No. 433 Corpl W Jones	" "	
4/4/02	No. 434 Corpl C Jope	" "	
	and 97 privates N.T.G. Batt.		
4/4/02	Sergt Burger and 16 men	2nd N.B.S.	
		O'OKIEP	
9/4/02	Intell. Scout Neale	F.I.D.	
	and 2 privates N.T.G.B. and 2 Intell. Scouts		Coloured
12/4/02	No.6262 Sergt Richard Arthur	5th Batt. War Regt.	
	and four volunteers		Native
20/4/02	Intell Scout Wm. Cook	F.I.D.	
	and one Intell. scout		"

RETURN OF ESTIMATED BOER CASUALTIES DURING THE OPERATIONS ROUND AND IN THE VICINITY OF O'OKIEP

		Killed	Wounded	Captured
31st March	Grootkau	3	3	
April	Springbokfontein	3	10	
April	Nababeep	3	2	2 surrendered rebels
April	Concordia	-	2	2 wounded
April	O'OKiep	15	50	
		24	67	

Shelton had every reason to believe the above to be a fairly approximate estimate of the enemy's casualties while engaged in the Siege of O'OKiep, and the operations in the vicinity from 31st March to 2nd May, 1902.

signed. Lieut. Colonel
Commanding Defence Force
O'OKiep 3rd May, 1902.

Appendix B

THE CAPE COPPER COMPANY RAILWAY

This was a two foot six inch gauge mineral line, ninety one and a half miles long and ended at Okiep in the centre of the mining triangle. On the other end of the line towards the west coast was Port Nolloth where the Copper Company transported its valuable ore. It was a Cornishman who had been hired by the Cape Copper Mining Company in 1869, one Richard Thomas Hall, who during the year 1849 was the Superintendent of the Chasewater and Redruth railway in Cornwall. His vast experience of narrow gauge railways (the best suited for conveying mineral ore) was to prove invaluable to the requirements of the Copper Company. On the 4th September, 1869, the first rail was laid at Port Nolloth which was to be the start of a new permanent way to the mining town and its neighbouring villages. Hall had carefully studied the difference in the terrain from the seaport inland across the sandy desert where the coastal area gradually became a granite plateau of rugged countryside climbing to the highest point of the Klipfontein Mountain (3,104 ft). Once on the summit the valley southwards fell away towards the mining centre at Okiep. The work was not easy and necessitated careful laying of the sleepers which were to hold the weight of the rails upwards to the summit of the great mountain. Hall decided on an unusual two foot six inch gauge railway to wind its way over the top of this highest point thereby allowing the trucks and the few passenger wagons to run downwards by gravitation to the Okiep mining community and the terminal of the line.

Hall used iron rails for each section weighing eight to twelve kilograms. At this particular time no steam engines had been introduced to pull or shunt the ore trucks and small passenger coaches of varying types. Instead the company used mules which were formidable little animals full of lasting strength, although at times stubborn. The Namaqualand Mule Train became well known not only locally, but further afield such as Cape Town and different parts of the world. On the 1st July 1876, the railway was completed and ready for regular operations.

The Copper Company had sixty mules to pull their train. These were divided up into groups of six to pull two mineral trucks and three mules to handle the passenger coaches. The Mule Train used to leave Port Nolloth early in the morning pulling passengers and stores of equipment. Departing at 6am they arrived at Anenous around 1 pm. Operators and passengers stayed the night at the Klipfontein Hotel situated at the top of the pass, departing next morning at 8am to complete the last stage of its journey to Okiep. It was the only rail link to Okiep and brought, not only vital equipment, but mail and necessary provisions for the community.

The Cape Copper Company Railway was, thanks to Hall, a great success and was followed in the 1890's by the use of steam locomotives which were put into service on the line and by 1893 steam working was complete through to Okiep.

The best engines for this purpose were built in the Kitson Works in Leeds, Yorkshire.

Appendix C

Copy of Letter intercepted by Shelton's intelligence agents from one Huligard B. Steyn, indicating Boer sympathizers were operating in German South-West Africa.

"Kakamas 30.4.01

My Own Fondest Darling

Can you ever believe that I am writing to you from this place? The last letter I wrote you was from the Aberdeen District, and this one from the world's end. We came to assist the Kenhardt Burghers, as well as the Calvinia Burghers, so we took the opportunity to come to the German territory so as to get some letters and important reports through to Europe, as well as to you. Oh my darling, you can never imagine what a treat it is again to give vent to my feelings. My previous letters were merely to let you know that I was still in good health. I can never tell you how I am longing for you, but what on earth is the good of longing, when it is impossible to meet. Anyhow I hope we shall some day be together again and make up for all the lost time, not so, sweetest? Ja Mijn Kind, since last we were together I have gone through many narrow paths, and am daily going through them. God has helped me thus far and I am positive he will protect me further. I hope dearest that you won't worry about me, always be cheerful - alles zal recht komen. I have heaps to tell you, but will wait until we meet, which I hope won't be long. How is dear old Lente? Kindly give her my best love, also to the other girls and your dear mother.

With heaps of love and fondest kisses
Your own and only
(signed) Huligard

P.S. I shall be glad to hear from you at an early date. Please address Huligard B. Steyn on one envelope and place it in another and address it to D.N. Liebenberg, Schuit Drift, PK Warmbad Duitsch Zuid West Africa. I have arranged further; so I am sure they will reach their proper destination.

Heaps of love
yours (H.S.)"

This letter was sent to Colonel Shelton who ordered that a copy be taken of it and sent through the normal channels.

Appendix D

Tribute to the late Henry Robert Moffatt Esq.
Ex Chief Civil Engineer - South African Railways

The author would like to pay tribute to the late Henry Robert Moffatt Esq., whom I had the pleasure to know through many exchanges of correspondence relating to the Cape Copper Company Railway which features prominently in this book.

Through the kind co-operation of Mr. Moffatt and much encouragement from him over many years in the past, while I carried out extensive research into the Namaqualand Railway, it was possible for me to piece together a comprehensive history of that important link from Okiep to Port Nolloth during the dark days of the guerrilla campaign.

I am sad that the late Mr. Moffatt will not be able to see the results of this extensive research and can only hope that perhaps some of his existing relations and friends may read these chapters.

*The **Pioneer** Engine*
By courtesy of the late Mr. Moffatt

Appendix E

During a lull in the fighting General Maritz, after consulting with some of his men, suggested to Col. Shelton that they might play a football match against the O'OKiep Garrison.   However, when Col. Shelton signalled this proposal to Col. Cooper - the following message was received:-

"From Co. H. Cooper, Klipfontein   Col. Shelton O'OKiep

NR April 29.. Your message re football match received. Regret that exigencies of service do not permit of this.

     By Helio 29.4.02.
                           signed H.C.

N.S. April 29..   Your message received will do what I can to help you. Hope infantry will reach me tonight ends

     By Helio 29.4.02.
                           signed H.C.

Stamped District Office May 2nd 1902   O'OKiep Namaquland

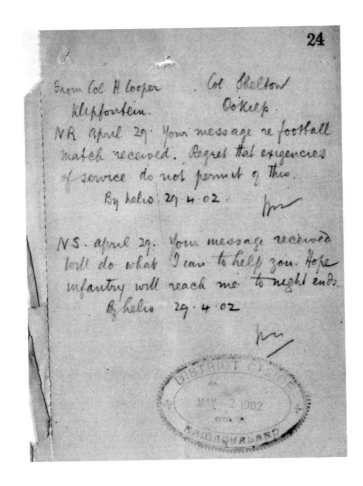

APPENDIX F

The other commando units who fought in Namaqualand were under the command of the following;

Bezuidenhout,

Malan,

G.C. Smith,

Conroy,

Golding,

A. Louw,

Theron,

Schoeman,

Van Niekirk,

Lategan,

De Villiers,

Neser,

Du Toit,

Lundt,

Stenekamp,

Boshoff,

Naude.

Total - 2400 to 2700 men.

Dedication

This book is dedicated to Lieutenant Colonel Shelton DSO 3rd Battalion Royal West Surrey Regiment (The Queens), Commandant of the vast district of Namaqualand, Cape Colony, South Africa and the soldiers of his Battalion, especially when on mobile patrols throughout the area. The men of the 5th Battalion Royal Warwickshire Regiment, the Cape Garrison Artillery, Namaqualand Border Scouts and the O'OKiep Town Guard.

The members of the Cape Copper Company's Railway. All black runners and intelligence scouts, the entire garrison of O'OKiep including the women and children for experiencing great hardships and for making many painful sacrifices during the eighteen months of the guerrilla warfare within their area and later during the Siege of O'OKiep. Also Colonel Cooper and his men of the British relief force who were strongly supported by members of the Kings Royal Navy.

In addition to the foregoing of the Boer and 'Volunteer Army', Assistant Commandant General Jan Smuts, Generals Van Deventer and Maritz and all the Boer commando units who were assisted by 'local' black scouts and volunteer troops when operating over vast distances during the classic and daring journey of their leader General Smuts to infiltrate the British held Cape Colony. Also for their endurance and tenacity in fighting a large proffesional army who eventually persuaded them to realise that to continue the hostilities would have been a futile effort.

This book is dedicated to all the foregoing men, women and children who were involved in this 'unnecessary' war - regardless of race, creed or colour.